J. WALTER MALONE

The Autobiography of an Evangelical Quaker

Edited by

John W. Oliver

Introduction by Arthur O. Roberts

NIVERSITY
PRESS OF
AMERICA

Lanham • New York • London

Copyright © 1993 by
University Press of America®, Inc.
4720 Boston Way
Lanham, Maryland 20706

3 Henrietta Street
London WC2E 8LU England

Library of Congress Cataloging-in-Publication Data

Malone, J. Walter.
J. Walter Malone : the autobiography of an evangelical Quaker /
edited by John W. Oliver ; introduction by Arthur O. Roberts.
p.   cm.
1. Malone, J. Walter.   2. Quakers—United States—Biography.
3. Malone College—History.   I. Oliver, John W. (John Walter)
II. Title.   III. Title: Autobiography of an evangelical Quaker.
BX7795.M225A3   1993   289.6'092—dc20   93–2204 CIP
[B]

ISBN 0–8191–9207–4 (cloth : alk. paper)
ISBN 0–8191–9208–2 (pbk. : alk. paper)

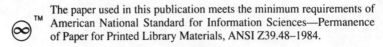

The paper used in this publication meets the minimum requirements of
American National Standard for Information Sciences—Permanence
of Paper for Printed Library Materials, ANSI Z39.48–1984.

For Marge Oliver,
Kim Oliver, John Oliver III,
Amy Lewis, Andrea Lewis,
and Malone College
with love

CONTENTS

J. Walter Malone

PREFACE

Miracles are never a stumbling block to the realist. . . . The genuine realist, if he is an unbeliever, will always find strength and ability to disbelieve in the miraculous. . . . If the realist once believes, then he is bound by his very realism to admit the miraculous also.
— FYODOR DOSTOYEVSKY, *THE BROTHERS KARAMAZOV*

THE MANUSCRIPTS

J. Walter Malone's autobiography was written in the early 1920s. The first draft was scribbled - the writing is almost illegible - in pencil in a loose-leaf notebook, and a typed copy was produced on which Malone did some editing. The two manuscripts were never completed, perhaps because of a traumatic event (the death of Emma Malone in 1924?), or because he was prevented from writing after being crippled by Parkinson's disease in the 1920s. Both documents are in the Malone College Archives.

In editing, I have maintained the flow of the narrative, but also taken care to protect the integrity of the stories and message. I have added the title,[a] footnotes, endnotes, subheadings, and insertions of names and dates into the text that are enclosed in brackets. My intent has always been to preserve the flavor of Malone himself.

WHY READ THIS STORY?

For Quaker history, the value of this autobiography lies in the contributions of the Malones to Quakerism. An earlier Quaker, Erroll Elliott, saw them pioneering a movement west of Philadelphia that "saved Friends Meetings . . . from near extinction," yet, after Elliott, the Malones were overlooked by historians. It is only recently that a younger scholar, Thomas Hamm, has noted that the Malones are "easily the two most important figures in evangelical Quakerism in the last one hundred years." Consequently, Malone's journal is a source for a watershed of Quaker history - it is what Douglas Gwyn calls "a major reference point for late nineteenth and early twentieth century Quakerism, in much the same manner as the journals of Fox and Woolman . . . for the seventeenth and eighteenth centuries."

---

[a]Malone originally entitled this work "Lifestories." I have changed the title to *J. Walter Malone: The Autobiography of an Evangelical Quaker* because I wanted the title to communicate quickly to a potential reader what this book is about.

J. WALTER MALONE: LIFE STORIES

For students of American religious history, Arthur Roberts suggests in the Introduction to this autobiography that Walter Malone was a "progressive evangelical" Quaker who achieved a "synthesis" between "personal holiness and . . . efforts for social righteousness." if, in our day, some stereotype Christians as either pietists or activists, while others separate private and public morality, it may be that open-minded readers in both groups will find Walter Malone's autobiography fascinating, and challenging, reading.

QUESTIONS

If Roberts is correct, as I believe he is, in seeing this synthesis of personal holiness and social righteousness as a significant event in western religious history, how is this integration to be explained? What was the antique pre-modern worldview that opened the Malones to visions of Christ, Satan, demons, and a throne in heaven, and impelled them to try to "rescue" the poor through "soul winning" and social action? Could this fusion of Holiness piety and social concern have been communicated to "modernist" Quakers, or was this synthesis only possible because the Malones were outsiders to an increasingly secularized religious mainstream?

ACKNOWLEDGMENTS

I want to express appreciation to professors Dale King, James Stuckey, and John P. Williams, Sr., who read this manuscript and made many helpful suggestions. I thank the J. Howard Pew Foundation, the Christian College Consortium and Coalition, and Provost Ron Johnson for funding, without which this work could not have been done. Finally, I am grateful to my able student assistant Craig Thompson for compiling the Index, John Rivers for computer assistance, Nancy Speers of Swarthmore College for genealogical helps, Marty Howard for photography, Linda Brantch for secretarial assistance, and Marlene Abrahamson, Hugh Barbour, Betty Bartlett, Edwin Bronner, Charles Cherry, Buffey Gillespie, Douglas Gwyn, Thomas Hamm, Larry Ingle, Ina Kelley, Noelle Libb, Barbara Mudrak, Marge Oliver, Kim Oliver, John Oliver III, Byron Osborne, Sr., Byron Osborne, Jr., Olive Osborne, Mary Ann Renner, Arthur Roberts, Martha Rodak, Robert Swierenga, Stan Terhune, David Tillman, and David and Geraldine Williams for helps or encouragements during this research. All errors, of course, are mine.

INTRODUCTION
by Arthur O. Roberts[a]

As defined by an earlier connotation of a now badly battered word, Quaker leaders J. Walter and Emma Malone were evangelical, that is, they offered their lives on the altar of spiritual sacrifice for this conviction: that persons can inwardly and redemptively experience Jesus Christ, who was crucified and resurrected in Jerusalem. They believed that the Christ thus inwardly experienced as Savior and followed as Lord brings persons to personal holiness and leads them into efforts for social righteousness and to global missionary witness. The American religious ethos of Protestant orthodoxy gave a context to these convictions; the social trauma of the Civil War era occasioned a wide-spread penitent yearning for holiness and a passion for evangelistic outreach.

J. Walter Malone's journal that John Oliver has edited and annotated, if read thoughtfully, offers helpful connotations for the word "evangelical." It is thereby instructive to contemporary readers for whom that word may have become so stereotypical of religious narrowness as to be rejected. Early in the text, for example, one finds mention of Malone's mother as a minister, whom he yearned to emulate, and of his submission to the discernment of women elders concerning direction for his own life. Such a portrait of an evangelical Christian community of faith stands in sharp contrast with certain recent "evangelical" movements which displayed marked resistance to women as ministers. Another example. Although Malone succeeded financially partly as a result of prayerful spirituality, he did not flaunt his wealth but remained sensitive to others, and was increasingly generous, and died poor. He viewed his wealth as a stewardship rather than a special privilege for the spiritually minded. In keeping with the ethos of the times this generosity took the form of compassionate help (of the "rescue mission" type) combined with personal evangelism, rather than efforts to overturn structural evil. In this way his evangelical piety was more like later fundamentalism than the neo-evangelicalism that followed the

---

[a]Arthur Roberts is a professor emeritus from George Fox College in Newberg, Oregon, and the editor of *Quaker Religious Thought*. Roberts has written many works on Quaker history and religion.

J. WALTER MALONE

turbulent Viet Nam years.

During the 19th century many Christian theologians, against winds of contemporary scholarship, sought to bind into coherent unity those doctrines that affirmed both the historic Jesus (as authoritatively witnessed by Scripture) and the experiential presence of Christ within the soul. For Quakers such as the Malones, doctrinal formulations did not weaken inward spirituality, but validated it, and fortified believers against a growing skepticism by scholars (including biblical ones) concerning the supernatural, the historicity of Jesus, and the dependability of Scripture. Words for these evangelicals were not stumbling blocks but rather beacons for spiritual wisdom and discipleship.

Evangelical Quakers of this era were wary of liberalizing trends in theology. In this wariness they were supported by respected and able British Quaker ministers whose pastoral visits and publications sustained their American brothers and sisters in the Christ-centered legacy handed down by 17th century Quaker forebears. The Great Separation of 1827 was a painful memory in many families, including that of Emma (Brown) Malone. These orthodox Friends considered that the more liberal "Hicksite"[b] branch of Friends had overstressed the subjective - the inward Christ - to the neglect of the historical Christ. This imbalance, they believed, led to an erosion of spirituality. They were less concerned than Friends would be later that the evangelical "Gurneyite" Quakers might lose the immediacy of divine presence and become "notional" fundamentalists bewildered over Quietistic language about "following one's Guide" or listening to the "inward Teacher." They did not envision a substitution of dogmatic test for discerned spirituality. Theirs was an orthodoxy, but an evangelical, or experiential one.

That is why at the Richmond Conference of 1887 delegates were pleased to include in their doctrinal affirmations a 1671 letter Fox wrote to the Governor of Barbados about Christ Jesus, the "alpha" and "omega," who becomes the shepherd of souls. The passage is marked by a sturdy Biblical apologetic, and reflects an early Quaker fusion (not easily sustained) of traditional Christian theological understanding and inward personal spiritual experience. This epistle assured Fox's[c] contemporaries of the general Christian orthodoxy of the Quakers. It also reassured harassed Friends of the historic grounding of their experiential faith. In times of trouble outer

---

[b]For the Hicksite background of Emma Malone see chapter 4.

[c]George Fox (July 1624 - 13 January 1690-91) was the principal founder of Quakerism.

x

certainties reinforce inward convictions. So it was that 19th century American Quakers found these outer certainties a bulwark to their experience in a time of national troubles and cultural uncertainties.

The Malones were in the forefront of a significant spiritual renewal among 19th century Quakers which was fueled by British evangelicalism and American revivalism. Quakers accommodated themselves to American revivalism uneasily and unevenly, but accommodate they did. A Quaker historian, Thomas D. Hamm, aptly titled his definitive study of this era *The Transformation of American Quakerism*. An earlier quietism gave way to an exuberant activism more akin to 17th than to 18th century Quaker practices. Solemn silent worship by a few gathered Quaker families deferred to largely attended meetings noisy with singing, preaching, and penitential praying. This activism stimulated a transition from a traveling to a settled ministry-- the pastorate system. But the new activism also fostered organized programs in missions, peace, and temperance. Progressive rather than conservative, the movement opened Quakers to wider ecumenical involvements such as Bible Societies, Christian Endeavor, and the Student Volunteer Movement.

Some Quakers became so caught up in the Holiness movement that sprang from American revivalism that they abandoned their historic family connections and joined new denominational groups, such as the Church of the Nazarene. Their departure was often justified on grounds of the "modernistic" direction taken by those Quakers who were reluctant to join in revivalistic enthusiasm. And those Quakers who resisted the new modes of worship and service sometimes justified their own departure from traditional Quaker orthodoxy on grounds of the excesses of the revivalists.

Such polarization drove some Friends to a more conservative stance-- they found revivalists and modernists alike too programmatic. They retreated to quietist ways, preserving the old testimonies about plain speech and dress, maintaining close community, and avoiding organizational entanglements. Tensions between progressive and conservative Friends resulted in several small separations into what are now known as the Conservative yearly meetings. But most Quakers of this era accepted the renewal and the reformation of church life. They allowed revival fires to inflame their smoldering Quaker heritage, to consume the dross of acculturated conventions and to refine the gold of transcultural values. So they added revivalistic methods to historic customs of worship and service, and were surprised by an astounding ingathering of new persons, unmatched in numbers since the 17th century. Here in America, too, was "a great people to be gathered."

Malone's journal provides evidence for this synthesis by progressive evangelical Friends. Persons involved with the Malones in publications and educational ventures were active in evangelistic efforts to save souls and in public efforts at social reformation. In this connection it should be noted that the evangelist Dwight L. Moody was a pacifist, the ancient Quaker testimony for peace found support in the evangelical-Holiness milieu prior to World War I.

But the synthesis was hard to sustain. After World War I the modernist-fundamentalist tensions in Protestantism hardened into distinct polarities. Those liberals who wanted to make the world safe for democracy through war were chastened, turned pacifist; and fundamentalists who had resisted war as unChristian, awed by the dimensions of human depravity, turned pessimistic about all human striving. Dispensationalist prophecy offered them a contrasting (if escapist) alternative to the naive liberal espousal of Social Darwinism ("the ape in man is about to die"). Jesus would soon return and bring in the Kingdom.

After World War I, the Holiness movement became shallow in its Kingdom focus and increasingly legalistic. Its theology became less ecumenical and more Wesleyan, and, as preached in camp meetings and churches, more doctrinaire about the nature of the conversion experience. Thus many Quakers abandoned Fox's "one work of grace" theology (which included both pardon for and cleansing from sin, but paid little attention to a time line for redemptive experience) for a neo-Wesleyan "two works of grace" theology (which separated the act of being saved from the act of being sanctified). It also meant that "holiness" Quakers focused more upon the inward work of sanctification than upon the outward moral implications of Christ's righteousness imparted to the believer. They were more eager to affirm sanctification as an instant purgative event than as a life of Spirit-guided holiness. They tended to forget "the Presence in the midst" in their preoccupation with a conversion sequence.

As a result of these changes the Holiness movement gradually lost force, and after World War II became decreasingly important to Friends. In the religious turmoil following that war, Quakers found evangelical ecumenical support from renewal movements such as the National Association of Evangelicals, Billy Graham crusades, Young Life, Youth for Christ, Basic Youth Fellowship, and World Vision. These movements were largely Calvinistic; they did not endorse Wesleyan holiness theology. Neither did they buttress Quaker testimonies such as pacifism or gender equality in ministry. In some ways these movements challenged Quaker distinctives more than did the earlier Holiness movement. For some Friends, therefore, the void left by the drying up of Holiness revivalism was filled by participation in modern charismatic movements, which reinforced the Quaker concern for direct and experiential empowerment by the Holy Spirit.

Introduction

Challenges to Quaker identity were faced by more liberal Friends as well, in particular universalist doctrines and ethical relativism (moral permissiveness) that eroded their social testimonies.

To meet such challenges, Quakers from all branches returned to their roots in a remarkable burst of historical scholarship. This in turn precipitated several renewal movements, including Faith and Life Conferences of the 1970's. These movements helped Quakers recover a new evangelicalism, instructed by the past but eager for a renewed witness to the world. They also brought divided Quakers into significant dialogue with each other.

But I have reached beyond the Malones' era to hint at a developing restatement of the dramatic synthesis they espoused. The circumstances in the Malones' lifetime that contributed to that later development must now be noted.

An important turning point in Quaker history occurred when the Malones declined to join other Quaker ministers in starting a theological seminary in Chicago, but decided rather to develop a Bible Institute in Cleveland. One may speculate. What if the Malones had put their resources into the Chicago venture and thus enabled it to succeed? What if Earlham College had accommodated itself less grudgingly to the revivalistic fervor of the day instead of reaching toward more liberal Protestant theology? What if revivalism had retained a broader, more ecumenical theology? What if the Malones had been poor instead of wealthy? In any case, "the road taken" by the Malones became an alternative route for Quaker education and leadership. For nearly a century, Bible colleges competed for students and support with Quaker colleges, and together they polarized people through contending loyalties.

Bible schools developed along the model of the Malones' Bible Institute from Ohio to Indiana, Iowa, Kansas, California, and Oregon. The metamorphosis of these schools is instructive. Friends Bible Institute and Training School, begun in 1892, subsequently became Cleveland Bible Institute, then Cleveland Bible College. Upon removal to Canton, Ohio, it became Malone College, named for its founders. A Bible School in Oskaloosa, Iowa, which became Vennard College and then Kletzing College, competed with Penn College. Friends Bible College at Haviland, Kansas, established in 1917, competed with Friends University at Wichita a hundred miles away, and with Nebraska Central College to the north. In 1990 it was renamed Barclay College. Huntington Park Training School for Christian Workers, begun in 1890 shortly after nearby Whittier College, subsequently became Pacific Bible College and then Azusa Pacific University in combination with a Free Methodist college with a similar history. North Pacific Bible Institute in Oregon became Portland Bible Institute and later Cascade

College. Cascade's closing in the 1960's reflected a renewed support by Northwest Friends for George Fox College, which had been founded as Pacific College in 1891. Union Bible Seminary at Westfield, Indiana, competed with Earlham, as did Taylor University and God's Bible School in Cincinnati. In North Carolina, John Fletcher College, offering a Wesleyan Holiness perspective, vied with Guilford College in the preparation of Quaker leaders.

Between 1892 and 1990, Bible schools broadened their curricula, and became, or yielded their Quaker leadership to liberal arts colleges. The Malones' leadership in this Bible school era is significant. Quaker leaders trained at Cleveland Bible Institute held significant positions of leadership among American Friends. For example, Edward Mott taught at Cleveland Bible Institute. He was an admiring protege of Walter and Emma Malone and William P. Kirby. Subsequently, Mott served many years as president of Portland Bible Institute and also as Clerk of the Oregon (now Northwest) Yearly Meeting. He served as a convener for a 1927 conference held at Cheyenne, Wyoming, aimed at finding ways to lift up a standard of evangelical faith which they felt had been eroded by liberal thought within the Society of Friends. The Great Depression and World War II hindered their efforts to gather a national conference. In 1947 this conference occurred, the first of a series of what was known as The Association of Evangelical Friends. For the keynote speaker, the aged Edward Mott, this conference constituted a personal validation. He urged a reaffirmation of the Richmond Declaration of Faith as a basis for Quaker renewal. He wanted the evangelical synthesis to hold.

Other persons from the Bible schools were also leaders of this movement, among them Byron Osborne from Ohio; William Kirby from California; Edward Mott, Walter Lee, and Earl P. Barker from Oregon; Scott and Grace Clark from Kansas; and Simeon Smith from Indiana. The influence of the Bible schools, through its education and its publications, was certainly evident, directly, or indirectly, in leaders such as Milo Ross and Charles Ball, then president of George Fox College and William Penn College, respectively, and Lowell Roberts, professor and president of Friends University, and pastors and superintendents such as Gerard Dillon, Lloyd Hinshaw, T. Clio Brown, Chester Stanley, and Dean Gregory. But the conferences reached beyond the context of the Bible schools, engaging public Friends such as Delbert Vaughn, Lloyd Cresman, Everett Cattell, T. Canby Jones, Eugene Coffin, and Arthur O. Roberts. From the non-pastoral tradition came Marian Baker and Dean Freiday.

The Association of Evangelical Friends became a catalyst for renewal for Friends from independent and united yearly meetings in the Orthodox tradition from 1947 to 1970. At the St. Louis Conference the Association was laid down with a sense of mission accomplished. By this time the Quaker colleges were strong and in touch with each other, independent yearly meetings had formed the Evangelical Friends Alliance for purposes of mission and publication cooperation, the Friends United Meeting had been restructured, and the Friends World Committee for consultation had become a vehicle for Quaker dialogue among all Friends. Evangelical Friends were no longer a defensive group but a part of a diffuse Quakerdom finding its focus, articulating the Gospel vigorously within that milieu, while affirming a cherished heritage and fostering mission worldwide.

Although Quaker Bible schools have disappeared from the North American scene, a rich legacy remains. That this is so, in significant measure, may be attributed to the vision and energy of J. Walter and Emma Malone.

Chapter One

MOTHER[1]

Mary Ann (Pennington) Malone (1885)[2]

"And I hungered to be a preacher like my mother was."[3]

Childhood of Walter Malone

Born August 11th 1857 on a farm in Clermont County, Ohio, not far from Cincinnati,[4] of pious and Godly Quaker parents, especially mother. who was a very loving, saved, and Spirit-filled woman, aggressive in religious matters, and wanting everyone to have the same happy experience that she had. Her ancestors[a] were along the line of William Penn and Sir Isaac Penington of early Quaker history,[5] with some of the blood of French Huguenots in her veins.[6]

Speaking of mother's religious experience, she had a very exceptional one, for she appeared to have a prophetic spirit. The Lord seemed to talk to her, or at least He seemed to answer her prayers in such a way that she often knew very definitely what was going to happen and just when things were going to happen. For instance, just about the time when I was born, mother was praying for a new home, as she was living in a small log house with her family of six boys and one girl.[7] Mother, amongst other things, when asking for a new home, told the Lord that this log house did not become a family of children of His, and was not as good a home as she thought she should have. She told her Lord that He could not afford to let her rear her large family in such a place, and not only did she want a good home, but one in a community where there would be church and school advantages.[8]

The Lord soon answered her, and very definitely. She was a very busy housewife and mother, with a family of seven or eight children, living in a small house, and with little time or opportunity for secret prayer, except at night, so she was used to making the early morning hour just before daylight her trysting hour[b] with her Lord.

One morning in that watch hour she pressed her case with tears and cryings to her Lord and Master: till, in fact, the answer came and He told her through the Spirit, "Today thou shalt have thy petition answered. I will send a man to thy home that has just the home thee asked for and needs." This message from the Lord turned her tears into rejoicing, which aroused father[9] from his sleep, and she at once gave him the good news. He appreciated the promise given to her, and he rejoiced with her. Father never seemed to hear from heaven

---

[a]Both Walter Malone and Levi T. Pennington, who was Malone's second cousin and a former president of George Fox College in Newberg, Oregon, were mistaken in thinking that they were descended from Isaac Penington. For materials on the English Pennington ancestry of Walter Malone, see endnote 5.

[b]"Trysting hour" may have a romantic ring, but the phrase is not out of place for pietists who feel a keen affection for God.

himself, but he always appreciated it when Mother did.[c]

The family had an early breakfast that morning, I guess. Meanwhile, mother, who was busy in the home, kept one eye up the lane which led from the house to the public road. At about one o'clock in the afternoon, a stranger stopped at the gate and drove up the lane. Mother met him at the door. After they had exchanged a formal greeting, he told her about his errand. He explained to her that he had a very nice brick house of eight rooms that was located on the Cincinnati pike at the edge of a nice village, Boston [now Owensville], Ohio.[10] She said to him, "I have been looking for thee all morning." He soon found out what kind of a Christian experience she had, and arrangements were soon made for us to move into this lovely home, which just suited mother's taste, and where we lived for eight years or more.[11]

Walter Malone's childhood home in Boston (Owensville), Ohio.[12]

---

[c]John Carl Malone, who was both the husband and the first cousin of Mary Ann (Pennington) Malone, appears as almost a supernumerary in this document. This may be due to Walter Malone's profound respect for the spiritual leadership of his mother, and to the fact that John Malone died fifteen years before the death of Mary Ann Malone. For information on John Malone, see endnote 9.

Unfortunately, while mother was pleased with her home in Boston, she was not satisfied with the family's circumstances in that town. This was because there were no Quakers there, and so of course there was no Friends meeting in this town for us to attend,[d] and we were all Quakers. So Mother talked matters over again and again with her Lord and Master, emphasizing the Scripture text - "That giving doth not impoverish Thee nor withholding enrich Thee."[e] She told the Lord that her family needed as fine a home as they had in Boston, but that the home should be located close to a good Quaker meeting. This was because it was important to mother to live in a Quaker neighborhood or community in which she could raise her family.

The Lord answered her prayer, of course. One evening, while we were sitting before an open fire in the living room in Boston, after family worship, I think it was, I saw the answer to mother's prayers come in the shape of a gift of ten one thousand Dollar bills,[f] which were laid in mother's hands [by Hezekiah Pennington Malone],[13] with the words "Buy a home of thy own for thy family."

It was soon after this that mother and father found themselves settled and living in as good a home as they had had in Boston, but a home which was near to the village of New Vienna in Clinton County.[14] It was here that she set up their family altar upon which God sent His fire. This home was indeed located in one of the finest Quaker neighborhoods[g] in all Ohio.[15]

---

[d]The Boston period was the second time that this Malone family had lived apart from Quakers and from the close-knit Pennington family: the first time was from 1844-1852 when they had left the Sandy Spring Meeting at Hanoverton, Ohio, to live on a farm in Portage County, Ohio. Mary Ann's dissatisfaction with Boston may not be due only to religious concerns for her children, but also to apprehensiveness over John Malone's breaking Quaker rules by joining and serving as Noble Grand Master of the Boston Lodge of the International Order of Odd Fellows, which is a secret society. See endnote 11.

[e]I cannot find this verse in Scripture.

[f]This is the first event in this autobiography that Walter Malone recalls having personally witnessed as a boy. Seven years of age in 1864, he was old enough to remember this incident.

[g]Walter Malone does not overstate the significance of the small southwestern Ohio village of New Vienna, which in the later 19th century was an extraordinarily
(continued...)

Walter Malone's boyhood home in New Vienna, Ohio[16]

One more event illustrates how the Spirit was in her heart, and how He answered her prayers. One summer day I saw mother come in the house from the garden, throw off her sunbonnet, hurry into her bedroom, and shut the door behind her. After an hour or more she came out with red tear-bedimmed eyes, which told a story of an intercessory scene with her Lord. In a careful way, and with a boy's natural curiosity I asked, "What is the matter Mother?" She answered, "Harry, who was one of her oldest sons, was in great danger somewhere and somehow, but God answered and saved his life. He's all right now. Oh praise the Lord."[17] At this time, Harry was in the far south. Letters received a few days later told how on that day, and at just that hour when mother prayed, he was caught by an undertow while in the ocean bathing, was carried off his feet, and "by a miracle"

---

[g](...continued)

important center for Quaker publishing, evangelism, education, and peace work. It appears to be no coincidence that Malone later became a contributor to each of these areas of religious and social concern. For the importance of New Vienna for Quaker history in the later 19th century, see endnote 16.

in answer to his mother's prayer he was placed on his feet again.

Living, as I did, in such a home, and with such a Mother praying, it was the natural thing for me to be alone in the barn or orchard praying in my heart too. And I hungered to be a preacher like my mother was. I was always asking mother religious questions, and when ministers were in our home, which was frequently, she would open the way for me to ask the question of them.

I do not know just when I was converted. Mother saw to it that each of her children had a spiritual crisis[h] and, again when older, another. I had special crises again and again, but I cannot tell in which of these I was converted, but I do know that I was born from above and sanctified by the incoming of the Holy Spirit. He took up His abode in my heart as the monument of Mother's prayers.

I attended [public] school at New Vienna until I was about fifteen or sixteen,[i] when I went from home to Earlham at Richmond, Indiana.[18] But my sister, Alice [Terrell], who was married [to Dr. Pleasant Terrell] and living in Cincinnati,[19] and my brother Harry,[20] who was in business there, wanted me to come there and go to school and graduate from the Chickering Institute in 1877.[21] This I did, and after graduation I obtained a position in the Pearl Street Wholesale House where I worked for three or four years.[22]

Cleveland

Mother was never very comfortable with my being in Cincinnati,[j23] and she had, from time to time, visited Cleveland where she attended the little Friends meeting that was held in the home of James and

---

[h]The phrase "spiritual crisis" is suggestive of the impact that revivalism was making on midwestern Quakerism in the 1860's and 1870's.

[i]One of Malone's teachers in the public school in New Vienna was Allen Terrell (d. 1892). Terrell later taught at Earlham College, and served as clerk of Indiana Yearly Meeting.

[j]Malone worshiped in Cincinnati for about three years with Levi Coffin (1798 - 16 September 1877), "president" of the Underground Railroad. See endnote 23.

Meribah Farmer on Superior Avenue,[k] where the Hollenden Hotel now stands.[24] Afterward, however, the Friends had built a neat and comfortable meeting house on Cedar Avenue[l] in the hope of getting their young people interested in the meeting, but it was too late by that time. They had all gone into the world so far it was impossible to get them back.[25]

For some years, a few elderly Friends had held a First Day morning meeting, but they seldom had over half-a-dozen in attendance.[26] And, as James Farmer told me once, he often sat through the morning hour alone. When he did not go to the meeting house, the building was opened and closed without anyone in attendance except the janitor.

This was about the state of things when I was led, undoubtedly by the Lord and in answer to my mother's prayers, to leave Cincinnati and remove to Cleveland.[27] My brother, Harry, in the meantime, had sold out his business in Cincinnati, married,[m] and had settled in Cleveland where he went into the business of quarrying stone with his uncle.[28] Not making very good - or not enough to support two families - the uncle [William D. McBride] had sold his interest in the business to my brother to be paid for as fast as he could out of the business. Harry was alone in the office, and he wanted me to come and take charge of the office, keep the books, etc., giving me $15.00 per month and a home with him in his family, which was all that the business could stand at that time.

This was the state of circumstances when mother again visited Cleveland, and attended the First Day morning services at the Friends meeting house on Cedar Avenue. The Holy Spirit at this time gave

---

[k]The Farmer residence where the Cleveland Friends Meeting began was described as "the grandest home in Cleveland." See endnote 24.

[l]The grey sandstone Friends meeting house in Cleveland was built in 1875 on the north side of Cedar Avenue and to the east of Blair (later 33rd) Street. Cedar is to the south of - and runs parallel to - Euclid.

[m]L.H. ("Harry") Malone married Carolyn Jayne Quayle on 13 January 1875. Carolyn Quayle was the daughter of Thomas and Eleanor Cannon Quayle. Thomas Quayle was a shipbuilder who came to Cleveland from the Isle of Man. One of Quayle's ships was the *Commodore*, which was the largest vessel (2082 tons) on the Great Lakes in the 1870's. In the later 19th century Cleveland was the largest center for shipbuilding in the United States.

her, while she was preaching to that little group of Friends, an inspiration and a prophetic vision in which she saw a great outpouring of the Holy Spirit bringing a gracious revival. She told them that she saw through the Spirit that the Cedar Avenue meeting house would one day be filled with happy throngs of worshipers, even to the enlargment of the meeting house and to the building of new buildings.

Mother's vision so surprised some of the elders that they took her to task for it after the meeting, for it seemed to them that she was letting her imagination run riot.[29] But, through her tears and her smiles, she assured them that it would all come to pass, and soon too, for she had been shown great things through the Spirit of which this meeting was the center.

J. Walter Malone (c.1877-1880)[30]

About this time I came to Cleveland,[n] and at once I became a regular attender at the Euclid Avenue Congregational Church, an

---

[n]Walter Malone came to Cleveland in 1880, where he resided with L.H. ("Harry") and Carolyn (Quayle) Malone at 861 Logan Street, which was close to the Euclid Avenue Congregational Church (now the Euclid Avenue United Church of Christ). The site of the home is now occupied by the Cleveland Clinic.

active worker in the Young People's meeting, and was put at my first Christian work teaching a boys' class.[31] The class had run two or three teachers off, and the last teacher left a week before I took it. The Lord gave me good success in this my first work for Him, and it encouraged my heart greatly, for the Lord had been dealing with me, and He had led me to give up much of my worldlinesss such as going to the theatre, never having gone a single time after coming to Cleveland.[32]

One day, I cannot recall how long after her vision at the meeting house, mother came into the living room where I was sitting and said, "Walter, I want to read thee something from the Bible that the Lord showed me this morning." "What is it about, Mother?" was my reply. "About Nehemiah building the walls of Jerusalem." "No," was my playful response. "I don't want to hear about that," for apparently the Lord had been talking to me about it. But of course she read and told me the story, and then - as only a Spirit-filled servant of God who had her eyes open could - she said that the Jerusalem she was talking about was that dead little Friends meeting on Cedar Avenue, and the Nehemiah who was to build the walls and the broken down places was J. Walter Malone. That personal sermon and message from my Mother was something that I never could get away from. I tried to laugh it away, and said to her, "Mother, I am not going down to that little Quaker meeting. I am doing good, and I am going to attend the Euclid Avenue Congregational Church." Her loving reply was, "Yes thee's going, and God will greatly bless and use thee, for He is going to do a great work there."

Shortly after this my brother Harry, with whom I was making my home, bought a lot and built a home [on Euclid Avenue]° within easy walking distance of the little Friends meeting house, and two or

---

°One enthusiast, Bayard Taylor, a noted world traveler, saw Euclid Avenue as the most beautiful street in the world, a street whose grandeur surpassed that of the Champs Elysées in Paris, Unter Den Linden in Berlin, and Prospekt Nevsky in St Petersburg. On Euclid Avenue, Walter Malone lived one block from the founders of Western Union, General Electric, and Standard Oil: Jeptha H. Wade was a director of eight railroad companies and founded Western Union, Charles F. Brush invented the arc light and founded the Brush Electric Company which became General Electric, and John D. Rockefeller founded Standard Oil. For a decade or so after coming to Cleveland, Malone took his lunch at the Union Club, where these leaders also gathered. This was quite a change from the crowded log house in which Walter Malone was born at Marathon.

three miles from the Congregational Church.[33] So naturally, one lovely Sabbath morning I felt my heart greatly drawn to go down to the Friends meeting. It was a warm and lovely morning, so several came out to the meeting, perhaps eight or ten of us. At the close of meeting, while all were visiting together and in no hurry to go away, an elderly Friend [Jane (Hussey) Pettit or Sarah Bye (Pennington) Langstaff][p] took me by the hand and said,

> Walter Malone, I am very glad to see thee this morning, and I have a little message on my heart which I feel is from the Lord. I feel that He would have thee attend meeting here and take charge of the Mission Sunday School that meets in the basement room on First Day afternoons.[34]

I thanked the Friend for the message, and she said for me to wait on the Lord about it and see what He would have me to do.

This Friend had not gone from me before another one in a plain Quaker bonnet who was also a minister [Meribah (Butler) Farmer or Hannah (Butler) Tatum][q] took me by the hand and said politely almost in the same words, "I feel that I have a message from the Lord for thee, Walter Malone. That thee attend meeting here and take charge of the mission Sunday School in the basement First Day afternoon which the present superintendent is about to give up." The first Friend saw me smile and broke in by saying to the second one, "I was just giving Walter the same message." Both of them assured me that neither had spoken to the other or to any one else, but only to me in the meeting house.

While we three were still talking, a third messenger, who was a man minister [David Tatum], joined our group, taking me by the hand, and he too said that he had a message from the Lord that I

---

[p]Jane (Hussey) Pettit (8 January 1812 - 8 November 1895) was a sister of copper industrialists Joseph G. Hussey (2 June 1817 - 27 March 1888) of Cleveland and Curtis Grubb Hussey (11 August 1802 - 25 April 1893) of Pittsburgh (who married Rebecca Updegraff), and the widow of Dr. William Pettit (Mary Ann's teacher in a Quaker school in New Garden, Ohio, in the later 1820's). Sarah Bye (Pennington) Langstaff (b. 18 February 1809) was Mary Ann's sister.

[q]Meribah Butler Farmer, a minister, wife of James Farmer, and a Cleveland philanthropist, always wore a Quaker bonnet. Hannah (Butler) Tatum, who was originally from Damascus, Ohio, was also a minister in the meeting at this time.

should attend meeting here and superintend the afternoon Sunday School.[35] We all smiled, and the first two said to the third that they had just brought me the same message. They again assured me that the message came first from my Heavenly Father. No one of the three had thought or talked of it. So my Mother's message, and my own feeling, were confirmed by the mouths of three witnesses. I assured them that I would consider it prayerfully. They were very anxious as the Christian Science people were already making overtures to rent or buy the place, and the Friends thought they could not keep it through another winter. I went home to dinner with a burden on my heart.

After dinner I could not rest, for I felt impelled to go down to the meeting house again and visit the little mission school. To my surprise, the discouraged superintendent up and publicly resigned his office. He then asked me to take it as a Friend, which he knew that I was. It seemed to be the only natural thing for me to do, and I followed this leading and accepted the position as my trust from the Lord. I was into this work almost before I knew it.

A Young Christian Worker

Following the Sunday School, at four o'clock there was a small gospel meeting held in the Sunday School which was also put into my hand to conduct. This soon became known as the Young Peoples Meeting.[36] All this work that was thrust into my care drove me to my knees for prayer and Bible study. I took this work as from the Lord. I took all the problems to the Lord, and He answered prayer.

The Sunday School sprang into new life. As I recall, one Sabbath the first month the attendance was seventeen, another Sabbath, twenty-five, another thirty-five, and another forty-nine, and up the enrollment ran until it was about five hundred.[37]

The Young People's meeting was as greatly blessed as was the Sunday School, and it grew in size and power until it was a veritable revival fire, so that for a year at a time there was an altar service every Sunday afternoon. Hundreds were converted and sanctified in these meetings, and they came from all parts of the city.[r]

---

[r]German names began to appear on the membership list of the Cleveland meeting in the 1880's. Quaker meetings in the United States were traditionally
(continued...)

Soon after the beginning of this work the question of finance came up. I did not like to ask people for money, but I needed it for Sunday School papers, song books, and the like. So I was very definitely led to pray for the Lord to bless the stone business so that I could pay for the needs of the Sunday School and the Young People's meeting. Of course I had prayed much over the business since going into the office and the work was very perceptibly picking up and going much better. I was led out into prayer for more stone orders and for collections to come in as it was for the Sunday School and Young People's meetings.[38] And it seemed to me as if I had no secular work. It was all for God and His work. I was in the stone business to pay expenses to further the religious work.

One day with the office door locked while in prayer and reading my little pocket Bible, I know not how, but I was led to the story in the twenty-eighth chapter of Genesis where the Lord so graciously met Jacob that night on the plain so far from home and from mother, and God gave him a new start in life. And I followed Jacob in his prayer and promises, underlining with pen and red ink each sentence of his vow to God, and thus making it my own prayer. It was my meaning to make the vows mine:

If the Lord will be with me, and will keep me in the way that I go, and will give me bread to eat and raiment to put on so that I come again to my father's house in peace; then shall the Lord be my God: and this stone which I have set for a pillar shall be God's house and of all that thou shalt give me I will surely give the tenth unto thee [Genesis 28: 19-22].

I went through the verses, underlining each part until I came to the last clause of the last verse, "And of all thou shalt give me I will surely give the tenth to Thee." Here I paused and was face to face with the tithing question for the first time in my life that I could recall. I had never heard it discussed that I knew of, nor knew anybody who did it. I was asking finances of the Lord, and He asked me to recognize His

---

ʳ(...continued)
composed almost entirely of Anglo-Americans. This was one of the first Quaker meetings - if not the first - to welcome large numbers of non-Anglos and the urban poor into membership.

demand if He gave money to me. While I hesitated, He began to give me promises of temporal blessing in such texts as these that my little pocket Bible fell open to:

God loveth a cheerful giver.

He shall receive one hundred fold in this present time.

Give and it shall be given unto you, good measure, pressed down and shaken together, and running over shall men give unto your bosom.

Honor the Lord with thy substance and with the first fruits of all thine increase: So shall thy barns be filled with plenty, and thy presses shall burst out with new wine.

And God is able to make all grace abound toward you; that ye, always having all sufficiency in all things, may abound to every good work.

This continued for some time until the pressure upon my heart was so great that I cried out "I'll do it Lord," and with this audible expression I took my red ink pen and underlined that clause with two lines for emphasis that said, "I will give a tenth to thee."

So I began tithing, thus planning and thinking that I would have some money to finance my Sunday School and Young Peoples meetings. When on the following Saturday I took $2.00 of my tithe for the first time and put it in my pocket I felt that I was a partner with God. But what was my surprise when in the Friend's First Day morning meeting the Lord impressed me during the silence so strongly that I should give those $2.00 to the minister who had preached, for he was a poor man and had no regular salary. I protested in my heart to the Lord, who was thus urging me to use the tithe as He was directing. I said, "This tithe is to pay for Sunday School papers for the boys and girls, and for singing books." The Lord replied, "I thought it was for me." I replied at once, "Yes, Lord, it is," and without waiting for the meeting to close I took it out of my pants pocket and put it into my vest pocket so that I could conveniently get it and slip it into the preacher's hand when I shook hands with him after the meeting as I had seen my father do when I was a boy at home. This was my first experience of handling the Lord's money, and I went home with a light heart to think that I was actually to be a partner of the Lord.

Toward the end of the week a gentleman came into the office and asked me to give him a little time and help that evening in a business way, and he would pay me for it, which I gladly did, and for this work he gave me $2.00, which was just the amount I that had given to the preacher. After I reached my bedroom and fell on my knees and thanked God for it, then I remembered saying to Him, "This was not giving to Thee when Thou gavest me just as much right back." And He said to me, "Did I not promise thee one-hundred-fold?" I was so happy over it all, I said, "Well, Lord, I'll just use this for the Sunday School." And I did, and I was happier still. Thus doubling my first tithe, I began the practice of tithing.

Within the next week the gentleman came back for help again, for which he paid me $5.00. Much of this money found its way into my tithing purse, for the joy was so great to have the Lord remind me that He had promised a hundred-fold. I told Him again that I was not giving Him anything. This went on each week until my income had more than doubled. I was never satisfied to give just one-tenth, and I soon learned that the more I gave to the Lord, the more He gave to me "good measure, pressed and shaken down and running over."

Thus it went on for perhaps six or eight weeks, but it was not over three months when, while I was reading my Bible one evening, which was my regular habit (the Bible was becoming so personal and precious to me, the veritable Word of God, and from which He was daily speaking to me), the Spirit began to speak to me and, before I arose from my knees, He told me that inasmuch as I had been faithful in a few things He was going to give me more, and that now He was going to give me one-third interest in the stone business of which now two of my brothers each owned one-half.[39] But I said, "Father, I have no money to buy it," and He said, "What is that to thee"? And I said, "Nothing, Lord, to Thee," and I thanked Him through my tears and I wrote my acceptance of one-third of the stone business on the margin of my Bible opposite the text through which He spoke to me. This was on December 19, 1881.[40]

When my heart was still enough and my spirit was quiet enough from praise and thanksgiving for this word and gift from Him, I at once arose and went downstairs and told my brother [Harry] all about the word of the Lord and His gift to me.[41] He believed my story, rejoiced with me, and praised the Lord with me.

We neither could see how it could come to pass, but that was not my business. The Lord gave me faith enough, which was the evidence of things not seen. Suffice it to say, it did come to pass just as the Lord had said, and within four or five weeks one-third interest in the company was in my name,[s] and the business made more money that year [1882] than in any previous five or ten years of its existence.[t]

And in my first year as a partner with the Lord I had the privilege of spending about $500.00 for Him as His representative. Not that I made ten times that much, but I was never satisfied with giving one-tenth of my income to the Lord. If there was a need, I was not careful whether it was out of the one-tenth or the nine-tenths. It was a delight for me to spend for the Lord.

---

[s]Walter Malone was a partner in the firm in 1882. On 26 August 1882 a lawsuit filed in the Common Pleas Court of Cuyahoga County, Ohio, listed Levi Harrison Malone, James Scott Malone, and J. Walter Malone as "**partners**" [emphasis added] doing business in the State of Ohio under the firm name of Malone and Co.

[t]Business did indeed improve. While chapter 2 tells more about the stone business of the Malones, some highlights can be seen from the following:
In 1874 Levi H. Malone opened a quarry in Euclid with Robert H. Maxwell and William McBride.

In 1878 this firm furnished the stone for sidewalks on the Superior Avenue Viaduct over the Cuyahoga River in Cleveland.

In 1882 Maxwell and McBride sold their interest in the partnership with Harry Malone to James Scott Malone. In this year J. Walter Malone also became a partner.

In 1883 the Malones were first listed in the Chicago City Directory as the Euclid Stone Company, and subsequently listed as Malone and Company and as the Portage Entry Stone Company.

In 1887 the Malones leased the Portage Entry Stone Quarry on Lake Superior near Jacobsville in the upper Michigan peninsula. Later in that year the Malones rejected an offer of $100,000 for a half interest in this quarry.

In 1888 the Malones opened a second quarry in Amherst township on the west side of Cleveland.

By 1892 the Malones were producing 1,050,000 cubic feet of stones per year: 250,000 at the Euclid quarry, 400,000 at Amherst, and 400,000 at the Portage Entry quarry, and they had offices in Cleveland, Chicago, and New York. For production figures, see the *Cleveland Plain Dealer*, 14 July 1892, p. 30.

In 1897 the Malone Stone Company sold their stone and railroad properties in the Cleveland area to the Cleveland Stone Company.

In 1912 the Malones gave up their lease to the Portage Entry quarries, and James Scott Malone became a general superintendent for the Cleveland Stone Company. He resigned in 1913.

For a partial list of buildings constructed with red sandstone from the Malones' quarry at Jacobsville, see the appendix at the end of chapter 2.

ENDNOTES

[1]This is the one chapter in this autobiography to which Walter Malone did not attach a title. I have presumed to entitle it "Mother"in honor of Mary Ann Malone.

[2]This portrait of Mary Ann Malone was painted by Florence Brown, who was a first-cousin of Emma Brown Malone.

[3]Mary Ann Malone was recorded as a Friends minister by Cleveland Monthly Meeting on 15 August 1889.

[4]Walter Malone was born on a 100 acre farm near Marathon, Ohio, that was located along the East Fork of the Little Miami River and Grassy Run Creek. See Clermont County Deed Book 58, Recorder's Office, Clermont County Courthouse, pp. 342-343. John Malone paid $2400 for this property on 11 November 1852. He sold the farm on 26 February 1863 for $4000, which was several years after the Malones had settled in Boston (now Owensville), Ohio. See Deed Book 77, p. 120. The farm is close to a historical marker placed by the Anthony Shaw Chapter of the Ohio Society to commemorate the "last Indian battle [in Ohio between] . . . Tecumseh, Shawnee Chief, known as 'Blazing Star' and Simon Kenton, a scout. . . ."

[5]For Levi T. Pennington's claim to descent from Isaac Penington, a Quaker pioneer and a son of a Lord Mayor of London, see Donald McNichols, *Portrait of a Quaker: Levi T. Pennington* (Newberg, Oregon: Barclay, 1980), p. 4. Instead, Walter Malone and Levi Pennington were both descended from Paul Pennington (21 September 1627 - 26 January 1719) and Ann Simpson Pennington (d. 9 February 1695) of Sunbreck, a hamlet that is located a few miles to the south of Swarthmoor Hall and near the shore of Morecambe Bay. Paul and Ann Pennington were members of the Friends meeting at Swarthmoor where they worshiped with George Fox and Margaret Fell. For Paul and Ann Simpson Pennington see Norman Penney, ed., *The Household Account Book of Sarah Fell of Swarthmoor Hall* (Cambridge: Cambridge U., 1920), pp. 270, 463, 475, 540, 545, 566. See also *Pennington Pedigrees: A Magazine for Pennington Cousins*, Vol. 12 (Fall 1980), pp. 2-3. Pennington family genealogical materials are in the Malone College Archives.

Regarding Judge Thomas and Margaret Fell, Walter Malone had a familial connection with the Fells. On 27 December 1843 Jane Cooper (a descendant of Judge Thomas and Margaret Fell) married Levi Pennington (Walter's grandfather) and became the only "grandmother" Walter Malone ever knew. For the genealogy of Jane Cooper Pennington see Charles Elmer Rice, *A History of the Hole Family in England and America* (Alliance, Ohio: R.M. Scranton, 1904). Jane lived to see the founding of the Christian Workers Training School (now Malone College) in Cleveland, Ohio, in 1892.

While Walter Malone was not related to Isaac Penington, a William Simpson from Sunbreck (a relative of Ann Simpson Pennington?) was one of the first Friends to present the Quaker faith to Isaac Penington. Simpson also donated the land at Sunbreck for a Quaker cemetery where Margaret Fell was buried. For materials on William Simpson see Norman Penney, ed., *The Journal of George Fox*, Vol. 2 (Cambridge: Cambridge University, 1911), p. 6. See also the "Manorial Court Rolls for the Manor of Munchland, the 14h Daye of the 8th Month called October 1658."

[6]Walter does not explain the basis for his claim to Huguenot blood, which may be based upon his descent from his great-grandmother Sarah Pettit Pennington (For Sarah Pettit see endnote 9). This claim does not appear in the typed version of this manuscript.

[7]The seven Malone children were Hezekiah Pennington (13 September 1841 - 20 January 1913), Alice Elvira (b. 21 August 1843), Charles Oscar (28 November 1844 - 10 June 1916), Levi Harrison (16 March 1847 - 18 December 1917), Edwin Theodore (1 October 1851 - 19 June 1922), James Scott (b. 6 June 1853), and John Walter (11 August 1857 - 30 December 1935), and William Lewis (b, 12 July 1859). Another daughter, Frances Emily, was born 31 August 1849 and died on 14 February 1851. Six boys (all of the above except for William Lewis) and one girl (Alice) lived in the Malone home at Marathon after Walter's birth in 1857.

[8]Mary Ann's boldness with God was not out of character for a strong-willed Quaker woman. See Barry Levy, *Quakers and the American Family: British Settlement in the Delaware Valley* (New York: Oxford University, 1988), p. 54.

[9]John Carl Malone (26 April 1813 - 17 January 1888) was the son of James Malone (8 November 1780 - 29 January 1835) and Sara Bye (18 March 1787 - 24 July 1830). Mary Ann Pennington Malone was the daughter of Levi Pennington (20 June 1784 - 26 May 1868) and Mary Bye (31 October 1782 - 7 July 1842). Sarah Bye and Mary Bye were daughters of Hezekiah Bye, Jr. (27 March 1754 - 20 June 1827), and Sarah Pettit (4 October 1758 - 6 September 1838). See Arthur Edwin Bye, *History of the Bye Family and Some Allied Families* (Easton, Pa.: Correll, 1956), p. 346.

James and Sara Malone married "out of unity" with the Buckingham Friends Meeting in Bucks County, Pennsylvania, but produced "acknowledgements" of wrongdoing and were received back into membership. John Malone was raised as an Orthodox Friend, but was excommunicated (Quakers say "disowned") by the Orthodox Friends Meeting at Buckingham for joining the Hicksites. John joined the Orthodox Quaker meeting at Sandy Spring (Hanoverton, Ohio) after his marriage to Mary Ann Pennington. Malone family genealogical materials are in the Malone College Archives.

[10]The "stranger" who invited the Malones to settle in Boston may have been Albert Redding: on 31 December 1862 the Malones purchased an eight-room brick

house in Boston with four adjoining lots from Albert and Nancy Redding for $3000. See Deed Book 77, Recorder's Office, Clermont County Courthouse, p. 229.

[11]The Malones moved from Marathon to Boston sometime between 1858, the year in which the Clermont Preparative Meeting that met in the Malone home at Marathon was discontinued, and 1860, the year in which John Carl Malone served as Noble Grand Master of Boston Lodge No. 189 of the International Order of Odd Fellows. For material on John Malone's leadership with the Odd Fellows see *History of Clermont County, Ohio, with Illustrations and Biographical Sketches of Its Prominent Men and Pioneers* (Philadelphia: Lippincott, 1880), p. 535.

[12]I am indebted to Shirley and Walter Shipley of Owensville, Ohio, for this picture of the Malone home in Boston (Owensville), Ohio.

[13]This gift came in the summer of 1864 when Walter Malone was seven years old. Byron L. Osborne, a son-in-law of Walter and Emma Malone and author of *The Malone Story: The Dream of Two Quaker Young People* (Newton, Kansas: United, 1970), p. 3, reports that the money came from Hezekiah (H. P.) Malone, the oldest of the seven Malone sons. I am indebted to Betty Bartlett, a granddaughter of H.P. Malone, for help with materials on her grandfather.

A $10,000 gift was no problem for H.P. Malone, who was employed in Cleveland in 1861 as a clerk with Joseph G. Hussey and William D. McBride, a firm dealing in shipping, copper, and oil. Hussey came from a Quaker background, and donated the land for the Cedar Avenue Meeting House. Joseph Hussey was a brother of the Quaker industrialist Curtis Grubb Hussey. For C.G. Hussey see Harrison Gilmer, "Birth of the American Crucible Steel Industry," *The Western Pennsylvania Historical Magazine*, Vol. 36 (1953), pp. 27-29. See also Dumas Malone, *Dictionary of American Biography*, Vol. 9, pp. 430-431.

The successful H. P. Malone first resided at 289 Prospect (the home of William McBride). By 1865 Hussey and McBride had become Malone, Pettit and Company, forwarding and commission merchants, with docks at 125 and 129 E. River Street. By 1866, after his marriage on 21 September 1865 to Emma Hart (a daughter of William and Elizabeth Kirk Hart), the firm of William Hart and Company became Hart, Malone and Company. Hart and Malone advertised as "the best furniture manufacturing house in the country," with sales of $200,000 a year. By 1868 H.P. was elected as director of the Buckeye Insurance Association which had a capital of $300,000.

From 1870-1873 H. P. resided at 467 Euclid Avenue. In 1874 he lived at 470 Euclid, which with renumbering became 1115 in 1875. In 1876 he lived at 847 Kennard, and by 1878 at New Vienna, Ohio. For Euclid Avenue in the later 19th century see Jan Cigliano, *Showplace of America: Cleveland's Euclid Avenue, 1850-1910*. (Kent, Ohio: Kent State University, 1991). For the families of Harry and Carolyn Quayle Malone and for Walter and Emma Malone on Euclid Avenue see Ella Grant Wilson, *Famous Old Euclid Avenue of Cleveland, At One Time Called the Most Beautiful Street in the World*. Vol. 2. (Cleveland: E. Wilson, 1937), pp. 187-189.

William Hart, the father-in-law of H.P. Malone, was president of Buckeye

Insurance and city treasurer of Cleveland for twenty years. Hart was unsuccessfully promoted by the *Cleveland Plain Dealer* (a Democratic newspaper) as a candidate for the Republican nomination for the state treasurer of Ohio.

Walter Malone is correct in saying that Mary Ann bought the home. John C. Malone's name does not appear on the deed. See Clinton County Deed Book 17, Recorder's Office, Clinton County Courthouse, p. 409.

[14]On 11 January 1865 Mary Ann Malone purchased a 109 acre farm on the northeast side of New Vienna, which included a brick home, for $12,825. Of this, $10,000 presumably came from H.P. Malone. $2,100 came from the sale of the property in Boston, Ohio. H.P. Malone signed as a witness to the deed for the new home. See Clinton County Deed Book 17, p. 409.

[15]The residences of the Quaker editor Daniel Hill (18 November 1817 - 16 November 1899) and Quaker publisher John M. Hussey (b. 6 February 1838) stood beside the Malone farm on its south side, and the home of the evangelist John Henry Douglas (27 November 1832 - 24 November 1911) adjoined the farm on its north side.

Publishing: In 1870 Hussey and Hill founded a publishing house in New Vienna next to the Malone farm. Hill was the founding editor of the *Christian Worker* and the *Messenger of Peace*. Both publications were later owned by the Malones. The *Worker*, the largest Quaker periodical in the United States, was merged by Walter Malone in 1894 with the *Friends Review* to found the *American Friend*, which under the editorship of Rufus Jones became the principal American Quaker periodical. It later became *Quaker Life*. Under the Malones, the *Messenger of Peace* later became the *Evangelical Friend*. In addition, Hill edited the *Olive Leaf* (a Sunday School publication with a strong peace emphasis), the *Bible Lesson Leaf*, and the *New Vienna Record*.

Evangelism: Douglas was the leading male Quaker evangelist in the later 19th century. Hill was also an evangelist, with a special interest in holding meetings for children - an interest that he shared with Mary Ann Malone.

Peace: Douglas was the first general secretary of the Peace Association of Friends. Hill served as President of the Peace Association from 1867-1869 and Secretary from 1869-1899. Hill also edited the peace section of the *American Friend* after its founding in 1894. For an example of Hill's concerns for peace and children see Daniel Hill, *The Books Our Children Read*, a booklet in the Haverford College Quaker Collection, p. 6, "Parents, look well to your libraries and the books your children read. Religious teachers, you may plead the merits of the blood of Jesus, but let not your garments be stained with the blood of your fellow-men."

Education: Douglas was the principal founder of Wilmington College, Wilmington, Ohio, and the first president of its Board of Managers. For materials on John Henry Douglas see Miriam Carter Douglas (Mrs. John Henry Douglas), "Facts Relative to John Henry Douglas' Work, Principally in the Years 1869 and 1870." Unpublished MMS in the Quaker Archives at Wilmington College, Ohio. See also Hugh Barbour and J. William Frost, *The Quakers* (N.Y.: Greenwood Press, 1988), pp. 311-312. In addition, *The Christian Worker* is an important source for articles by John Henry Douglas.

[16]I am indebted to Virginia Smith of Wilmington, Ohio, for this picture of the Malone home at New Vienna.

[17]Harry (Levi Harrison) Malone, may have been traveling for a Cincinnati firm in the later 1860's. In 1872 he was listed in the Cincinnati City Directory as president of Malone & Stahl, a business that manufactured and distributed sewing attachments.

[18]Walter Malone was a student in the Preparatory Department (High School) at Earlham College in the spring semester of 1874. He received a grade of "passing" in arithmetic, grammar, geography, and physical geography. I am indebted to archivist and historian Thomas Hamm of Earlham College for showing me a copy of Walter Malone's transcript for the spring semester of 1874.

[19]Alice Malone married Dr. Pleasant Terrell on 15 February 1871. Dr. Terrell died on 29 December 1880 at the age of 37. He is buried in the IOOF cemetery in New Vienna. For Alice Terrell see chapter 8.

In Cincinnati, Walter was part of an extended Quaker family that included his uncles William Harrison Malone, who was a younger brother of John Carl Malone and the president of the Mill Creek Lumber Company, and Hezekiah Bye Malone, who was a foreman with the lumber company. The family also included Ezra Bailey who built Earlham Hall, which was the first building at Earlham College. Bailey was the husband of Elizabeth Bye, who was a sister of Mary Bye Pennington (the mother of Mary Ann Malone and therefore the grandmother of Walter Malone). Another family member was James Langstaff, who was the husband of Sarah Bye Pennington (Mary Ann Malone's oldest sister). Bailey and Langstaff worked for W.H. Malone. One other family member was Lydia Bye Langstaff, who was Walter's great aunt and the widow of John Langstaff. The Mill Creek saw mill and lumberyard were located on the south side of Front Street and between Wood and Mill Streets.

[20]Three Malone brothers - Levi Harrison, Charles Oscar, and J. Walter - lived at 516 West Court Street, which was the home of their uncle William Harrison Malone.

[21]The Chickering Classical and Scientific Institute was founded in 1855 by Josiah Boutelle Chickering as a "Select School for Boys." Called "one of the best" private schools in the United States by the *Cincinnati Daily Gazette* in 1877, it enrolled 215 students in 1877. Walter was one of seventeen graduates in a class of only nineteen. The school's first seven graduates in classics went to Harvard or Yale. Two Chickering professors later taught at Yale. Walter no doubt majored in business. For material on Walter Malone at the Chickering Institute see *Catalogue of the Chickering Classical and Scientific Institute* for 1875, 1876, and 1877 in the Cincinnati Historical Society, Cincinnati, Ohio. Walter is listed as a "middle year"

student in 1875, a junior in 1876, and a senior in 1877. Catalogues for the years 1865-1887 are in the Cincinnati Historical Society.

[22]The Pearl Street Wholesale House was the popular name for Martin, Thieman & Company. The owner's son was a classmate of Malone's at Chickering. If the students were seated alphabetically, Malone and Martin must have been frequently together.

[23]In Cincinnati, Walter worshiped with his extended family at the Friends Meeting House at the northwest corner of Eighth and Mound Streets. In 1875 this meeting had 229 members, including Levi Coffin, Joseph Taylor (who endowed Bryn Mawr College in Philadelphia), and Mordecai Morris White (president of the American Bankers Association in 1893). Walter Malone got his first exposure to urban missions in Cincinnati. I am indebted to Atty. Thomas Hill of Cincinnati for a copy of Thomas J. Kiphart, *One Hundred Fifty Years of Cincinnati Monthly Meeting of Friends, 1815-1965*. For further material on the Cincinnati Meeting see the "Minutes of Cincinnati Monthly Meeting" and *Members of Cincinnati Monthly Meeting, First Month, 1st, 1875* (Cincinnati: Achilles Pugh, 1975). The two latter sources are in the Quaker Archives at Wilmington College, Wilmington, Ohio, where I was graciously assisted by Ina Kelley.

[24]The Cleveland Friends meeting began in the home of James and Meribah Farmer at the corner of Superior Avenue and East Sixth Street in 1871. The home was described by the *Cleveland Plain Dealer* at the time of its construction in 1856 as "the grandest" home in Cleveland. The Hollenden no longer stands on this site.
James Farmer (19 July 1802 - 17 March 1891), a descendant of Governor James Oglethorpe of Georgia, was president of Ohio National Bank and State National Bank, and founder and president of two railroads: the Cleveland and Pittsburgh, and the Valley Railroad. Meribah Butler Farmer (1805 - 4 April 1898) was a prominent philanthropist who served on the boards of the Cleveland Orphan Asylum, the Aid Society of the Civil War, and the Retreat (a Cleveland home for the mentally disabled). Mr. Farmer dressed in a broad-brimmed Quaker hat. Mrs. Farmer wore a Quaker bonnet. A grandaughter of the Farmers was the wife of John Griggs, the attorney general of the United States under President William McKinley. For James and Meribah Farmer see Lydia Ethel Farmer Painter, *The Memoirs of James and Meribah Farmer* (Cleveland: Whiteworth Brothers, 1900).

[25]One of the young people who had left the Friends was Alfred A. Pope, later president of the National Malleable Castings Company with plants in Cleveland, Chicago, Toledo, Indianapolis, Sharon (Pennsylvania), and Melrose Park (Illinois). Pope's mother, Theodate (Stackpole) Pope, was a recorded Quaker minister. For the Pope family see Ella Grant Wilson, *Famous Old Euclid Avenue of Cleveland: At One Time Called the Most Beautiful Street in the World*, Vol. 2. (Cleveland, 1937), pp. 120-123. Another former Friend who had left the meeting was the industrialist Joseph G. Hussey, who had employed Hezekiah Malone and donated the land for the Cedar Avenue Meeting House. In 1863 Hussey - who was

presumably no longer committed to non-violence - helped to escort General William Tecumseh Sherman to the railroad station after a triumphal visit to Cleveland. Another Clevelander who came from a Quaker background was Marcus Hanna, the United States senator from Ohio. Hanna's grandparents had been menbers of the Friends Meeting at New Garden, Ohio, where they had worshiped with young Mary Ann (Pennington) Malone. The Hannas, however, who sided with the Hicksites in 1828, had not joined with the Orthodox Friends in Cleveland.

[26]Walter Malone reported to the Conference of Friends of America in Indianapolis in 1892 that James Farmer wept openly when talking about his children. He reports Farmer's saying to him, "O my boy, if the day had only come sooner when my children could have been saved to the church . . . . We built this meeting house, but we were afraid to have anyone come."

[27]Walter Malone is first listed in the *Cleveland Directory* for 1880-1881 at 861 Logan, the home of Harry Malone.

[28]Levi Harrison ("Harry") Malone came to Cleveland in 1874, married Carolyn Quayle in 1875. and entered the stone business with his uncle William D. McBride, who had earlier brought H.P. Malone to Cleveland, and with Robert H. Maxwell. "McBride, Maxwell & Malone, miners and manufacturers of sawed flagging and building stone" is listed in the *Cleveland Directory* for 1875. Harry Malone lived in McBride's home at 1115 Euclid Avenue from 1875-1878.

[29]Mary Ann Malone was no stranger to the elders of the Cleveland meeting. James Farmer had lived as a boy beside Mary Ann's parents (Levi and Mary Bye Pennington) at New Garden, Ohio. As young adults, James Farmer and Mary Ann Pennington had been members of the Sandy Spring meeting at Hanoverton, Ohio. Another elder, Sarah (Pennington) Langstaff, was Mary Ann's older sister.

[30]I am indebted to Jean (Crobaugh) Merrick for this picture of young Walter Malone. Jean is a grandaughter of Walter and Emma Malone and a daughter of Margaret (Malone) Crobaugh.

[31]This Euclid Avenue Church was located close to the home of Harry and Carolyn Quayle Malone on Logan Street. While the relatively young Harry Malone may have had little in common with elderly Friends at the Cedar Avenue Quaker meeting, it also appears that both Harry and Walter Malone were following a pattern that was not uncommon at this time among Friends who were moving from rural Quaker communities to urban centers, which was to leave their Quaker roots and find a new church home in the city.

[32]Malone's view of his own "worldliness" in 1881 does not quite fit with an account by Nathan Frame, the husband of Esther Frame, who was the leading female Quaker evangelist in the later nineteenth century. Nathan Frame described Walter Malone as a "backslider and society man" when Malone attended a Quaker revival conducted by the Frames in January 1881 in New Vienna, Ohio. Indeed, as

a member of Cleveland's Euclid Avenue set, Malone was, without doubt, a "society man." A "backslider"? That must depend on one's frame of reference. The most serious offense that appears to have troubled Walter Malone's conscience at this time was having attended the theatre while in Cincinnati, a "sinful" practice which he claims to have stopped when coming to Cleveland. For the Frames' account of the restoration of this "backslider" in 1881 see Nathan T. Frame, *Reminiscences of Nathan T. Frame and Esther G. Frame* (Cleveland: Britton, 1907), p. 278.

[33]Walter Malone moved with Harry and Carolyn Malone to 1879 Euclid Avenue in 1881. Walter lived at this address from 1881-84. From 1884-1887 he is listed as living with James Scott Malone at 1144 Euclid, which he may have left after his marriage to Emma Brown in 1886. In any case, Walter and Emma were residing at 242 Kennard by 1888, and after this on Prospect Avenue, a street that runs parallel to Euclid on the latter's south side.

[34]The mission Sunday School had been founded by Thomas McKinney, a young blacksmith, who taught newsboys in his shop on Sundays. The class later moved to the Y.M.C.A. on Prospect Aveune where it was led by Caleb Davies. After this, the class met in the Friends Meeting House on Sunday afternoons. See Nellie S. Waterbury, *A History of First Friends Church of Cleveland, Ohio, 1871-1937* (Cleveland, 1937), p. 79. This work with the poor may have been an offshoot of an earlier work begun by David Tatum.

[35]David Tatum (1823 - 29 September 1912), was an evangelist, temperance worker, and social reformer, and the only recorded male minister in the meeting at this time. Tatum was superintendent of the Home for the Friendless in Cleveland, and active with the poor in the inner city. He was especially concerned for evangelism and temperance work, and went on missionary journeys to England, Scotland, Switzerland, Belgium, France, and Germany. For David Tatum see the *Autobiography of David Tatum: The Formative Years*, with an Introduction by Louis T. Jones (Indianapolis: John Woolman, 1963). Copies are in the Quaker Collection at Guilford College and in the Malone College Archives. For an obituary see the *Evangelical Friend*, Vol. 8 (25 October 1912), p. 7. See also chapter 5.

[36]Malone's use of the term "gospel meeting" when he wrote this in the 1920's is anachronistic for Quakers of the 1880's. Nevertheless, this sort of meeting suggests the receptiveness of the elderly Friends to evangelistic work with children.

[37]On 19 August 1886 the *Christian Worker* reported that Cleveland Friends had "been obliged to increase the quarters for their Sabbath School. They have rented a rink and have an attendance at the school of about five hundred and the number is increasing."

[38]I can find no record in the Cuyahoga County Archives of any suit by the Malone Stone Company to extract monies from a debtor. However, there was a suit in 1882 against the Malone Company in the Cuyahoga County Court of

Common Pleas by Adin Hendershot, who alleged that he had not been compensated for hauling sand. The case was "dismissed for want of prosecution without prejudice and judgment." The Plaintiff was required to pay the court costs.

[39]The owners in 1881 were Harry and James Scott Malone, two of Walter's older brothers.

[40]The *Chicago Directory* for 1883 lists the Euclid Stone Company, a Malone enterprise, with offices at 177 La Salle Street. The Chicago office was run by Edwin Theodore Malone and Philip B. Parker. Malone and Parker lived at 285 Bissell.

[41]In December 1881 Walter was living with Harry and Carolyn (Quayle) Malone at 1879 Euclid Avenue.

Chapter Two

HOW THE LORD LED IN BUSINESS QUESTIONS

"the Lord gave me my interest in the stone business. . . . and He was to be consulted in all of our transactions."

As indicated in the last chapter, [in 1882] the Lord gave me my interest in the stone business.[1] I was sure in my heart that He was interested in it and He was to be consulted in all of our transactions. So I often called my brothers to a season of prayer when any particular wisdom was especially needed, and I prayed without ceasing over orders and over collections of money to pay our bills and especially our workmen's payroll.

As an example of how the Lord at times guided me, the brother who ran the quarry told me that the quarry needed more orders as they were running short. Later, when in the office alone, I asked my Heavenly Father to have some of our customers send us an order today, and my mind seemed to settle on the Bay City Stone Company of Michigan. I pressed my need of it <u>today</u>, and I felt the answer through the Spirit that they would send us an order <u>today</u>. Whereupon I at once thanked Him for it, wrote it down on a sheet of paper, and put a statement on the sticker on the desk to the effect that the Bay City Stone Company would send us an order for stone today. I did this to show my brothers when they would come in, which was not until the next morning. Looking over the mail the next morning, sure enough there was a letter from the Bay City Stone Company and enclosed was an order for a few special large stones and a letter saying the rest of the order would follow within a day or two. Whereupon one of my brothers said, "The Lord hurried them too much."

Sidewalks

After we had opened an office in Chicago for the sale of stone,[2] there was a large city park sidewalk job up for bids that would be awarded to the lowest bidder. One of my brothers and my cousin [Philip B. Parker] who had charge of this office wanted this job very badly. When they telegraphed me to come up and help them get it, I responded and went. We had never had one of these large park jobs, and we were determined to get this one if possible.

The night before the bids were to be opened, we three had a prayer meeting for wisdom and guidance, but nothing came. In the morning we prayed again before going to our office, and in my spirit I never ceased praying and holding on for guidance as for the price to put in to get the job. The bids were to close at twelve noon, and at about 10 o'clock I went out to be alone until I should know what price to bid. While alone in the closet the Spirit seemed to whisper to me, "The lowest bid beside yours will be $.40 per square foot." "I sincerely thank Thee," I whispered, and at once hurried back to the office where my brother and cousin had given up on my returning and had already put in the bid. One said, "Well, we had given you up and have just written out the bid which must be in within a few minutes." I said, "What price did you quote"? He said "$.44 per square foot." My reply was, "The Lord just told me the lowest bid besides ours would be $.40 per square foot." They therefore at once withdrew the bid that they had written, tore it into pieces, and said that we would bid 39 cents. "No," I said, "we will bid $.39 and 7/8 cents, which we did. And when the bids were opened the lowest bid until ours was 40 cents. Ours was 39 and 7/8ths. The contract was awarded to us.

Another time in Chicago the boys in charge of the office were planning and trying hard to get a contract for the sidewalk around the new building of the Board of Trade on LaSalle Street. They had worked and figured and prayed. Our boys talked to the building committee about putting the walk in on stones reaching from the building to the curb, which would require many stones to be 21 or 23 feet long. At least it would take many stones longer than any that had ever been put in a sidewalk in the United States.

Euclid Railroad

The stone companies in Chicago did not want to lay it in one stone; we did. But our quarry was not on the railroad. We had to haul all our stones on wagons three or four miles to the railroad. So this job would require our company's building a railroad from the quarry some three or four miles to the [Nickel Plate] railroad. So the question of price to give to furnish these long stones in Chicago came up. We had prayer meetings over it time and again during which we besought the Lord to give us wisdom as to the price to give.

One day when I was having an audience with the King regarding the price to be named, the Holy Spirit made intercession for me and I felt privileged to press the case more than usual. Whereupon the Spirit fastened upon my heart the price of $23,524. In a moment I remember replying to the Lord and saying, "But Lord, I know they have a price $7000 lower than that." His reply was "What is that to thee? Follow thou Me." And I said, "I will Lord," and I did. There was a private company laying this sidewalk, which did not have to be obtained on the basis of competition or to the lowest bidder. Suffice it to say that we got the job at that price [in 1885]. But by the excess we got for special stones sent the price up to about $30,000,[3] of which $11,000 was practically clear profit, and with which we paid for the building of a railroad into our quarry, in the building of which God wrought more than one miracle for us.

Now that we had this big contract, we had to build a railroad into the quarry to get the stones out,[a] for they could not be hauled by wagons. Our competitor in this Euclid district [the Forest City Stone Company] had their quarries to the east of us on the banks of

---

[a]Wages at the Malone quarry on Nine Mile Creek in Bluestone (now South Euclid) to the east of Cleveland, ranged from 75 cents to $1.25 a day. The quarry's mill which cut stones into slabs was 150 feet long and 80 feet wide. It ran six gangs of saws, and used an Ingersoll steam drill that carried steam eleven hundred feet into the quarry and drove the drill into twenty inches of solid rock in three minutes. The mill was torn down in World War II and reused for scrap steel. Bluestone contained numerous shanties, two saloons, and a Temperance Hall (built in 1877) where we may suppose that Walter Malone (the "stoneman preacher") sometimes spoke. The quarry's whistle could be heard for miles around. For the Euclid quarries, see Anthony Palermo. "Bluestone, Cleveland's Ghost Suburb: A Past Remembered," typed ms., p. 9. A copy of this manuscript is in the Malone College Archives.

Euclid Creek. They were older men and experienced in the stone business, as well as in railroad affairs.[4] They had been talking for some years of building a railroad up that hill to their quarry. They had one or two railroad men as stockholders and directors, had made more than one railroad survey, and found it would cost between $90,000 and $100,000. They thought they would not be justified in building due to the cost. This fact threw a chill on the spirit of my older brother [Harry] who was president of our company.

However I was confident that the Lord would see us through. After leading us thus far, He would not allow us to be defeated. So I went to prayer about this matter. One night as I was praying for light on the next step it came to me through the Spirit that there was a gully up the hill in which we could build a railroad directly into our quarry for the amount of $25,000.

The next day I communicated this information to my brother who had charge of the quarry. He thought he knew that part of the country perfectly, for he was well acquainted with its topography. So when I told him that the Lord had a route for us where we could build for $25,000, his reply was, "Walter, thee is crazy." I said, "Well, Harry, I don't know anything more about it, but if thee will go out and spend a day or two searching it out thee will find it, for it is there in reserve for us." He acted on this advice the next day, and came back to the office a day or two later with a bright and cheery countenance and enthusiastically said, "I have found a way it can be done for $25,000." It was done, and the Euclid Railroad Company's account on our books when the job was finished showed the cost to have been $24,994.[5]

But getting the right-of-way and building the railroad was no easy task for three young men with very little money behind them. How we got the $25,000 to buy the right-of-way and build with I will not stop to tell, but will say it was just in answer to prayer like the rest. But the crisis came when the right-of-way was all bought from the quarry to the Nickel Plate Railroad with which we had made the arrangements to connect, except for one piece of property on Euclid Avenue which we had to cross. This owner put up a regular fight saying he would not let us cross for $10,000.

I cried and prayed for days and nights over it, and found no way of getting across his farm on the south side of Euclid Avenue. This was in the fall of the year, and the railroad had to be finished by early spring. It seemed as if we had to go to court to avail anything, but in going to court we would have to incorporate into a regular railroad company, get a charter from the state, incorporate, and become a common carrier if we were to have the right to condemn and take over private property. This prospect forced us to our knees more than ever.

I thought I could not go to law, and I could get no word from the Lord regarding it. But we decided that there was nothing else to do, and so we directed our attorney to take all the steps necessary for incorporation and to apply for a state charter as a regular railroad company, which he did. Then I saw for the first time why we had had to incorporate. We saw by the daily paper two days later that our competitors had applied for a charter for a railroad and were just arranging to condemn and buy our whole line of private right-of-way. Had it been two or three days later we would have lost all our opportunity for building a railroad.

Then we discovered for the first time that it was this competitor who secretly was causing us all the trouble with this last piece of right of way. Our competitor, after seeing that they were too late to get our right-of-way up the gully, then came out in the open to challenge in court our right to be a railroad company.

Now the court was to decide that question. By this time we had begun the grading to the road-bed. To buy and pay for the three or four miles of right-of-way, grade it for the track, and then not to have the court decide the whole matter in our favor would have wrecked our stone company as well as the railroad company. We only had four or five months, just time enough by continuous work to get it finished so that we could begin the Board of Trade job in Chicago.

So while the trial was going on in the court, there was great searching of heart and earnest prayer while the witnesses testified and the lawyers pleaded, for there were railroad lawyers of note on both sides. When the trial was finished the judge said he would want three or four weeks to go over the testimony and the lawyers' arguments. We could not wait for this, for our contract in Chicago must be begun before spring opened. We dared not go on further without a "Thus saith the Lord," and it was not long in coming.

The answer came to my heart as I was praying one evening on my knees before my open Bible and voicing my petition in an undertone, just having communion with my Lord. In some way, I know not how, my Bible opened to the 124th Psalm, which the Holy Spirit took up and began to talk to me and to apply to our case:

If it had not been the Lord who was on our side, now may Israel say;
If it had not been the Lord who was on our side, when men rose up
against us:
Then they had swallowed us up quick, when their wrath was kindled
against us:
Then the waters had overwhelmed us, the stream had gone over our
soul:
Then the proud waters had gone over our soul.
Blessed be the Lord, who hath not given us as a prey to their teeth.
Our soul is escaped as a bird out of the snare of the fowlers: the
snare is broken, and we are escaped.
Our help is in the name of the Lord, who made heaven and earth.

I do not know how the Spirit laid emphasis on the word "now" in the first verse. He told me from "now" it was all settled and we need not wait for the judge's decision. No anxious waiting. No longer a heavy heart. "Now." As to what we would do if the case went against us, the Spirit told me to begin to rejoice. So in verse two, when men rose up against us, when our competitors rose up against us, when they had swallowed us up quick, when their wrath was kindled against us, and on through this chapter the Spirit applied every verse and every line to our railroad case, and I praised Him with voice and tears for this assurance of victory in and through it all.

I soon found my brothers who were greatly burdened and heavy-hearted over the uncertainty, but were greatly comforted by my message from the Lord, which they believed as they always did. They asked me about the railroad building and said, "Shall we go ahead and build it over the right-of-way to the contested land on each side, trusting the Lord to put us through? I said, "Build the railroad up on both sides and God will put us through." But they said, "Remember it means bankruptcy and the loss of every dollar that every one of us has if we don't get through." But I still said to build it up to the line on both sides, and go ahead and do it now. We went at it and had much of it graded and ready for the rails by the time the court gave its decision, which was just as we asked for in every particular.

One more suit would have to follow, which was necessary in order to condemn the property of the man who had so strongly fought against us. However, before doing this, we first made him an offer of $1500 for the right-of-way to build the railroad across his property, which he promptly refused. He then brought a law suit against us in which he claimed $10,000 damages. The jury, after going out and looking it all over, came in and gave a verdict of $1495 for this right-of-way.[b]

It is enough to say that from that time on everything was easy sailing. We got the railroad finished, had the job in Chicago finished in good time, and got nearly $5,000 more than our original contract for extra work that was not in the contract.[6] And our fighting competitors were glad after the railroad was finished. They built a switch over to us so that they could ship all their stone over the railroad,[c] paying us well for the privilege, although when they were in court fighting to keep us from building it they had said under oath that this railroad was not needed and not wanted, and claimed that they would never use it, and neither would anyone else except the Malone Stone Company, a private business concern. But they forgot all this later.

---

[b]The spot on the Euclid Railroad that was built around this farmer's pig pen was subsequently known as "pig pen curve." For a nostalgic look at the Euclid Railroad, which continued to operate into the 1950's, see the *Euclid Sun Journal*, 14 May 1992, pp. C1-2. In the memory of one Euclid resident, "It was the only train in the world that stopped for cars."

[c]The Forest City Stone Company was established by W.H. Stewart and John Holland in 1872. In 1875 they purchased a quarry that covered forty-eight acres from Albert and James McFarland on the east bank of Euclid Creek. They later advertised that their quarry was "connected [by the Malone's Euclid Railroad] with the Nickelplate railway." See the *Cleveland Plain Dealer*, 14 July 1892, p. 30.

APPENDIX

The following is a list of some public and corporate office buildings - together with a few private homes from Walter Malone's neighborhood on Euclid and Prospect Avenue in Cleveland - that were constructed from red sandstone provided by the Malone brothers from the Portage Entry Quarries near Jacobsville, Michigan.[7]

ALBANY, NEW YORK
Hudson Canal Building

ANNANDALE,
MINNESOTA
Annandale Town Hall

BESSEMER, MICHIGAN
Gogebic County
Courthouse

BINGHAM, NEW YORK
Allen's Cigar Factory

BLAIR, NEBRASKA
Blair High School

BLOOMNGTON,
ILLINOIS
Bloomington High
School
First National Bank
Franklin School
U. S. Post Office

BUFFALO, NEW YORK
The Masonic Temple

BURLINGTON, IOWA
Burlington Public
Library[8]

CALUMET, ILLINOIS
Calumet City Hall
Elk's Club
Sacred Heart Church
St. Ann's Church
St. Mary's Church
St. Paul's Church

CHICAGO, ILLINOIS
Armour Buildings
Baptist Church, 56th
and Woodlawn
Church of Epiphany
Fourth Baptist
Hyde Park Baptist
Presbyterian Church
41st. and Grand
St. Paul's Lutheran
Universalist Church,
30th and Prairie
University Church,
Congregational
Washington Park
Congregational

CINCINNATI, OHIO
Carew Building
Y.M.C.A. Building

CLEVELAND, OHIO
Colonial Club
Hickox Building
Dr. Hobson's Assoc.
Lennox Apartment
Osborne Building
Pilgrim Congregational
Church
Society for Savings
Western Reserve
Building
Western Reserve
University,
Laboratory Bldg.
West Side Library
Y.M.C.A. Building,
Prospect and Erie

CLEVELAND: EUCLID
AND PROSPECT HOMES
Stewart H. Chisholm,
3730 Euclid (built
1891)
George B. Christian,
1643 Euclid
L. Dautel,
1759 Euclid
Elberin Apartments,
Euclid and Hilburn
Dr. Charles Parker,
1521 Euclid
Arnold C. Saunders,
7407 Euclid (built
1892-1894)
Mrs. W.H. Severance,
Euclid and Bolton

DANVILLE, ILLINOIS
Soldiers' Home,
Barracks

DAVENPORT, IOWA
United States Post
Office

DETROIT, MICHIGAN
Children's Free
Hospital
Detroit Business
University
First Congregational
First Presbyterian
Jefferson Ave.
Presbyterian
Masonic Temple
Union Depot at Fort
and 3rd Sts.[9]
Y.M.C.A.

DUBUQUE, IOWA
Dubuque High School

DULUTH, MINNESOTA
Board of Trade
Chamber of Commerce
Duluth City Hall
Duluth & Iron Range
Depot
Fowler Building
Jefferson School
Lyceum Theater
Saint Louis County
Jail
Torrey Building

FARGO,
NORTH DAKOTA
Elliott Hotel
Fargo City Hotel
Fargo Opera House
Red River Valley Bank
Waldorf Hotel

GALESBURG,
ILLINOIS
Central Congregational
Lesher Buildng
I.O.O.F. Building
Marquette Building
Y.M.C.A.

GRAND RAPIDS,
MICHIGAN
Briggs Block
M.J. Clark Building
Kourtlander Murphy
Wholesale Building
Michigan Trust
Peninsula Bank
Universalist Church
Wellington Flats

GREEN BAY,
WISCONSIN
East High School[10]

GREENFIELD, INDIANA
Columbia (Riley) Hotel

HAMILTON, ONTARIO
Normal College (later
part of McMaster
University)

HASTINGS, MINNESOTA
Hastings High School

HOUGHTON, MICHIGAN
Michigan Mining School

JANESVILLE,
WISCONSIN
Janesville High School

KALAMAZOO,
MICHIGAN
Adventist Church
German Workingmen's
Association
Kalamazoo High School
Michigan Central Depot
Masonic Temple

KANSAS CITY,
MISSOURI
Keith Building

KEWANEE, ILLINOIS
A. Hallin Building
A. McLean Building
Union National Bank

LA PORTE, INDIANA
Laporte County
Courthouse

LINCOLN,
NEBRASKA
Lincoln High School

LOUISVILLE,
KENTUCKY
The Commercial Building

LUDINGTON,
MICHIGAN
Mason County
Courthouse

MADISON, INDIANA
U. S. Post Office

MARQUETTE,
MICHIGAN
Kaye Hall (Northern
Michigan University.)
Marquette County
Courthouse
Union National Bank

MARSHALLTOWN,
IOWA
Marshalltown High
School

MEMPHIS, TENNESSEE
The Public Library

MINNEAPOLIS,
MINNESOTA
Globe Building
Kelly Flats
New York Life
Insurance Building
Northwestern Guaranty
Loan Building

MONMOUTH, ILLINOIS
Warren County
Courthouse

MONTGOMERY,
MINNESOTA
Montgomery Town Hall

MT. CLEMENS,
MICHIGAN
　Medea Bath House
　　and Hotel[11]

MUSKEGON, MICHIGAN
　Hackley Manual
　　Training School
　Muskegon County
　　Courthouse
　Occidental Hotel

NEW ORLEANS,
LOUISIANA
　New Orleans National
　　Bank

NEW YORK CITY,
NEW YORK
　Altman's New Stores
　Amphion Theater
　Army and Navy
　　Building
　Bleeker Street
　　National Bank
　Brevort Building
　Brooklyn City Bank
　Brooklyn Fire Dept.
　　Headquarters
　Fisk, Clark & Flagg
　　Building
　Hide & Leather Bank
　Lincoln Club House
　Manhattan Savings
　　Institution
　Montauk Theater
　Waldorf-Astoria Hotel
　Park Avenue Presbyterian

OMAHA, NEBRASKA
　Brenner Tenement
　　Block
　Kohlback Building
　Kurback Block
　Manning Block

New Fort Crook,
　Commissary Building
　and Officers Quarters
Omaha City Hall[12]
Pacific Express
　Building
Powell Block
Tenth Company Barracks
　and Mess Hall

PEKIN, ILLINOIS
　Tazewell Hotel

PEORIA, ILLINOIS
　Jewish Synagogue
　Peoria City Hall
　Peoria Public Library
　Rock Island Depot
　Sandmeyer Store
　Webster School
　Woolner Building
　Woolrich Building
　Y.M.C.A.

PETERSBURG,
ILLINOIS
　Menard County
　　Courthouse

PHILADELPHIA, PA.
　Academy of Natural
　　Sciences
　Bourse Building
　Woman's Hospital of
　　Philadelphia[13]

PITTSBURGH,
PENNSYLVANIA
　Carnegie Office
　　Building[14]
　Graff Building
　Herron Building
　Lincoln National Bank

PORT HURON,
MICHIGAN
  Busch Block
  Hotel Harrington
  St. Claire County Bank

RACINE, WISCONSIN
  U. S. Post Office

ROCKFORD, ILLINOIS
  U. S. Post Office

ROCK ISLAND,
ILLINOIS
  U. S. Post Office

SAGINAW, MICHIGAN
  Bank Building
  Masonic Temple
  Public Library
  Saginaw City Hall
  Vincent Hotel

ST. JOSEPH, MISSOURI
  Burnes Estate Office
    Building
  Commercial Block Office
    Building
  Donovan Hotel
  First Baptist Church
  Richardson, Roberts &
    & Byrne Building
  Tootle, Wheeler &
    Motter Building

ST. LOUIS, MISSOURI
  Globe Building
  Wainwright Building

ST. PAUL, MINNESOTA
  Arcade Building
  Elsinore Apartments
  Endicott Building
  German Children's
    Hospital
  Germania Bank

Germania Life
  Insurance Building
Major John Espey
  Central Block
Manhattan Building
  Manheimer Block
Marlborough Apts.
Pfeifer Block
New York Life
  Insurance Building
Ransom and Horton
  Building

SIOUX CITY, IOWA
  The Toy Building

SOUTH BEND, INDIANA
  Public Library

SPARTA, WISCONSIN
  Monroe County
    Courthouse

SPOKANE,
WASHINGTON
  First National Bank
    (later called Exchange
    Bank)

SPRINGFIELD, ILLINOIS
  Springfield High School

STRATFORD, ONTARIO
  Stratford City Hall

TERRE HAUTE,
INDIANA
  Terre Haute High School
    (later called Wiley)

TOLEDO, OHIO
  Toledo and Ann Arbor
    Depot
  Toledo Bee
  Toledo Club
  Ward School

TOPEKA, KANSAS
St. Joseph's Catholic
Church

TORONTO, ONTARIO
Board of Trade of
Canada
Canadian General Electric
Company
Chamber of Commerce
College Street Baptist
Church
Confederation Life
Conservatory of
Music
Cook's Presbyterian
Church
Dominion Permanent
Loan Company
Dunn Avenue Methodist
Globe Office
Gooderham Building
Gowans and Kent
Grosvenor House
Imperial Bank of Canada,
North
Jessup Building
Lawlor Block
Pugsley and Dingman
Wholesale Block
Bunting Reed
Wholesale House
Rooney and Company
Royal College of
Dental Surgeons
Sick Children's
Hospital
R. Simpson and Co.
University Chemical
School
University Gymnasium
Wycliffe College (the
theological college of
the Univ. of Toronto)
Y.M.C.A., West End
Y.W.C.A.

TROY, NEW YORK
Troy Orphan Asylum

UTICA, NEW YORK
St. John's Catholic
Church

WATERVLIET,
NEW YORK
St. Patrick's Church

WAYNE, NEBRASKA
Wayne County
Courthouse

WEST SUPERIOR,
WISCONSIN
Blaine High School
Board of Trade
Chicago, St. Paul,
Minneapolis, and
Omaha Depot

WHEATON, ILLINOIS
DuPage County
Courthouse[14]

WINNIPEG, MANITOBA
Dominion Bank Building

ENDNOTES

[1]The Euclid quarries of the Malone Stone Company were located at Bluestone (now South Euclid), Ohio, a few miles east of Cleveland. The quarries were first developed by Duncan McFarland. Robert H. Maxwell, who was a partner with William D. McBride and Harry Malone, was McFarland's son-in-law. Liberty E. Holden, owner of the *Cleveland Plain Dealer* and the Hollenden Hotel, was a major investor. The Euclid quarry employed Scots, Bohemians, Italians, Irish, and Swedes.

[2]The Malones were first listed in the *Chicago Directory* in 1883 as the Euclid Stone Company with an office at 177 LaSalle. The office was headed by Edwin Theodore Malone, the fourth of the seven Malone brothers, and Philip B. Parker. Malone and Parker lived at 285 Bissell.

[3]*The Daily Inter-Ocean*, April 25, 1885, reported that the Euclid Stone Company, Euclid, Ohio, was paid $24,700 for sidewalks for the Chicago Board of Trade building.

[4]The Forest City Stone Company was founded in 1872 by W.H. Stewart, W.C. Stewart, and John Holland. Their Euclid quarry, which comprised forty-eight acres, was located on the banks of Euclid Creek, and "connected with the Nickelplate railway [by means of the Euclid Railroad that was built and owned by the Malones]." See the *Cleveland Plain Dealer*, 14 July 1892, p. 30.

[5]Harry Malone was listed as president of the Euclid Railroad Company in the *Cleveland Directory* for 1886. Belvoir Boulevard now runs along the gully that the Euclid Railroad followed to reach the Malone quarry.

After building the Euclid Railroad, which ran for only four miles from the Euclid quarry to the Nickel Plate Railroad, the Malone brothers received passes that permitted them to travel without charge on the major American railroads - a courtesy or "perk" which railroad presidents extended to one another at that time. Descendants of the Malone brothers tell the story that on one occasion Harry Malone was traveling by rail from St. Louis to New Orleans, and seeing that the train would arrive late, telegraphed ahead the message that a ship on which they had planned to travel from New Orleans to Florida was not to sail until "Commodore Malone" was aboard. The ship, I am told, waited until he arrived. Harry had been granted the title of "Commodore" by the Dunedin, Florida, yacht club.

[6]The Euclid Stone Company's contract for $24,700, plus this extra $5000, suggests that Walter Malone was correct when he stated (see p. 29) that they got "about $30,000" for the job.

The *Chicago Directory* for 1885 incorrectly lists Walter Malone as president of the Euclid Stone company, but correctly notes that his home is in Cleveland. It lists E. T. Malone as Secretary and Treasurer. There is another listing for "Malone

& Company (E.T. Malone) stone, 36, 159 LaSalle." The Euclid Stone Company and Malone & Company were both Malone enterprises.

The *Earlhamite*, November 1885, reported "The Malone Stone Company is represented at Cleveland by Walter Malone, at Chicago by Will L. Malone, and at New York by Philip Parker - all old Earlhamites." William Lewis Malone was the youngest of the seven Malone brothers.

[7]For materials on the Malone's Portage Entry Stone Quarry see "The Portage Entry Quarries Company: Miners and Manufacturers of Portage Red Sandstone [and] Marquette Raindrop Sandstone." Copies of this booklet are in the library at Michigan Technological University and the Malone College Archives. See also Clarence J. Monette, *The History of Jacobsville and Its Sandstone Quarries*, pp. 56-65. Copies are in the Portage Library, Houghton, Michigan, and the Malone College Archives.

For reasons of space, I chose not to list private residences that were built from this stone, except for residences from Walter Malone's neighborhood on Euclid Avenue. However, two other homes that deserve special mention are the Richard Beatty Mellon mansion in Pittsburgh (1909) and the Horace E. Dodge home in Detroit (1912). For a history of the 65-room Mellon home at 6500 Fifth Avenue (which was completed in 1909 at a cost of $3,000,000 and "required almost 100 people to run"), see the *Pittsburgh Post Gazette*, 29 January 1972. The Mellon home was razed in 1940, and the red sandstones were used to build Mt. Saint Peter Catholic Church in New Kensington, Pennsylvania. The home of auto industrialist Horace Dodge, which was popularly known as Rose Terrace, was located on Jefferson Avenue near Grosse Point.

[8]The Burlington Public Library was restored and renovated in the early 1990's with red sandstone that was taken from the former Dubuque (Iowa) High School - stone that was also provided by the Malones. David Metzger, the architect for the project, reports that the only red sandstone of comparable color and cementitious properties is from New Delhi, India. In Metzger's words, we are "treating this sandstone like gold." I am indebted to librarian Susie Guest for materials on the Burlington Public Library.

[9]The Union depot, built at a cost of $1,000,000, was opened in 1893. It was a three story structure that stood 166 feet by 118 feet, with a corner tower 100 feet high. The exterior walls of pressed brick were trimmed with Portage Lake red sandstone.

[10]This stone from East High School was later used for the front (west) walls of Packer Stadium on the northeast corner of Walnut and Baird Street, which was at one time the playing field for the Green Bay Packers. The stone was also used for the arch over the entrance to the stadium. The gates and the arch have been torn down.

[11]Mt. Clemens was an important center for health spas in the later nineteenth and early twentieth centuries that featured mineral baths. The original Medea Bath

House was built in 1882, and expanded in 1891 into "one of the largest bathing establishments in the world, capable of giving 1,500 baths a day." The bath house and the Hotel Medea, which opened in 1904, were fronted by "ten massive arches . . . of Lake Superior red sandstone [which] enclose an arcade porch 180 feet in length by 16 feet in width. The same stone is used with red pressed brick in carrying up the entire front of the building, giving a rich and massive effect." See *Centennial History of Mount Clemens, Michigan, 1879-1979* (Mount Clemens: Mount Clemens Public Library, 1980), pp. 84-85. I am indebted to Mrs. Brown of the public library in Mt. Clemens and to Norman O. Lorway for materials on the bath house.

[12]The Omaha City Hall at the corner of 18th and Farnam Streets was completed in 1894 at a cost of $547,000, and was popularly known as "Old Red Castle." It was torn down in 1966.

[13]The Woman's Hosptal of Philadelphia is now called the Medical College of Pennsylvania.

[14]The Carnegie Office Building was later the corporate headquarters for the United States Steel Corporation. The Malone stones covered the outside walls up to the second-floor level. See *Engineering News*, January 11, 1894, p. 34.

[15]The DuPage County Courthouse in Wheaton, Illinois, was constructed in 1896 and 1897 at a cost of $75,000. Portage Red Stone was used in the base work and up to the window sills. The building was sold in 1992 to the National Lewis Educational College for $3,000,000. Dr. Lon Randall, a former president of Malone College, is now an administrator of the National Lewis College.

Chapter Three

FIRST QUAKER REVIVAL

"I said that I had a matter of importance to present to them."

In the meantime, my Christian work was growing in numbers and in power, and it was reaching out to a neighborhood that was a community of laboring men, carpenters, and various kinds of mechanics and clerks. It was just an ideal community for Christian work. The Sunday school [at the skating rink] grew rapidly into hundreds. The Young People's meeting was not far behind.

There grew at this time upon my heart a burden, or perhaps I should say that an old-fashioned Quaker concern took hold of me for the Friends' First Day morning meeting on Cedar Avenue where I regularly attended. At the close of one of these First Day meetings, the Friends decided to start a Bible study, which they asked me to conduct. This I gladly did, although I was practically the only one in the meeting who was not gray-headed. I was about twenty-five years of age at that time.

It was also about this time [January - February 1881][a] when I went on a visit to my parents' home at New Vienna, Ohio, where I was delighted to find Nathan and Esther Frame,[b] the far-famed Quaker

---

[a]The "revival" ran for five weeks until 27 February 1881. *The Christian Worker*, Vol. 11 (3 Third Month, 1881), p. 102, reported that "about 150 persons have professed conversion, or have been renewed from an almost dead state. . . . It is very rare now to see an intoxicated person on the street, or hear a profane word."

[b]Esther Frame was a woman evangelist in the later nineteenth century - to the *Cleveland Plain Dealer*, she was a "peerless Evangelist." Frame became a Quaker after being told by a Methodist minster that "it is all nonsense to think a woman is called to preach." Esther Frame and President Ulysses S. Grant were grandchildren of two McGary sisters. See Nathan T. Frame and Esther G. Frame, *Reminiscences of Nathan T. Frame and Esther G. Frame* (Cleveland: Britton, 1907).

evangelists who were conducting a blessed revival. While visiting with them, I took occasion to speak of the concern, as well as the opportunity, for a great revival in the Friends Meeting in Cleveland if we could only get the consent of the few Friends who attended. I told them I thought that if they, Nathan and Esther Frame, would write a letter to the Friends stating that they had a "concern" to hold a series of meetings with them, that the way would be opened for it. I told the Frames to send the letter to me, and I would read it to the Friends at an appropriate time, and I would explain that it agreed with a burden that I had had for some weeks.

A few weeks later, after the letter came from the Frames, and on the first pleasant First Day morning when the Friends were able to be in attendance at the Meeting House, I asked them all to tarry for a little while. I said that I had a matter of importance to present to them.

Of course they all stayed, and after some introductory remarks I read the letter to them and told them that this was our opportunity to have a gracious revival and build up our church, and that we could fill the meeting house and our Sunday School and our Young People's meeting. I asked them to gladly cooperate, for I felt that it was God's time to pour out His Spirit.

Instead there was quiet opposition. Some said it would not be after the good order of Friends. Others feared that there might be some singing,[c] or other exercises in the meeting that "we were not accustomed to." I told them that I expected there would be, but that unless they did something the meeting would soon die. Others thought that there was not a Friend's home in which the visiting ministers could be entertained, and other like excuses, till they concluded "the way does not open at the present time."

I went home with rather a heavy heart to pray that God would not let the conservatism of the elderly Friends defeat His will. After this, a great peace came into my heart regarding the matter.

Next morning, at about 11 o'clock, who should drive up in his elegant coach in front of our office to call but James Farmer, the wealthy and aristocratic Friend who sat at the head of the meeting, and whose word and wish were always the will of the meeting. After

---

[c]The Frames reported that Cleveland was "one of the 'old-time meetings,' and there had never been a hymn sung in it until we went there." See *Reminiscences*, p. 276.

a short visit he turned to me and said,

> Walter Malone, some of us could not rest easy with the decision of yesterday's conference regarding the coming of those Friends ministers, and some of us have given some further consideration to the matter. We have decided to tell thee that if thee thinks best, thee may write to them and invite them to come, and thee can find a good boarding house for them and take them there, and have the bill of expense sent to me and I will see that it is paid. And further, I feel like telling thee that thy being in our meeting with us and thy teaching in the morning Bible class following the meeting, and thy bearing in general has been so satisfactory that I feel like telling thee to just go ahead and do as thee feels led and I will stand by thee in it all. Just let me know what is the amount of the expense that thee thinks I should pay, and I will gladly pay it.[d]

So of course I praised the Lord for His good hand upon me. The letter was written to the evangelists, and all arrangements were satisfactorily made, and they soon came to Cleveland [March 1882]. The house was filled, and the first Quaker revival in Cleveland was on.

At the close of one First Day morning meeting on either the first or second Sunday morning of the revival, one of the elderly Friends put his arms around me, kissed my cheek, and said, "Now I am ready to depart in peace, for I have seen for the first time this meeting house filled with worshipers."

In this revival, there were perhaps between one hundred and two hundred professed conversions, and there were many Christians who claimed to have been sanctified and filled with the Holy Spirit. Very little was made of joining the meeting, as so little was known about Quakers in Cleveland. I think that after the revival had closed and a few new members were added, there were less than a score of new members when the new monthly meeting was set up from Salem, Ohio, to which meeting the Friends in Cleveland belonged.[e]

---

[d]The Farmers subsequently became friends of the Frames. While in Cleveland, James Farmer took Esther and Nathan Frame to visit Mrs. James A. Garfield, the widow of the former president. See *Reminiscences*, pp. 279-280.

[e]Cleveland Monthly Meeting was established on 13 April 1883. Prior to this time, the Cleveland congregation was a preparative meeting under the care of the Salem (Ohio) Monthly Meeting.

Emma Isabel (Brown) Malone in the later 1870's or early 1880

Chapter Four

MEETING EMMA I. BROWN

"I believe that woman would love me."

It was during this meeting [the Frames' revival in January - February 1881] that Emma Brown, a beautiful little Quakeress from the west side of the city [a district called Ohio City], began to attend the Cedar Avenue meeting house. It was here that Emma first became interested in the Friends meeting.

Quakerism was not new to Emma Brown, who had been reared [near Toronto] in Canada in an old Quaker neighborhood and in a Quaker home, but a home that had been split by the unitarian teachings of Elias Hicks.[a] Her father [Charles W. Brown][b], and also her grandfather [Ira Brown], sympathized very strongly with the Hicksite branch,[1] while her mother [Margaret (Haight) Brown] was a devoted Christian who sympathized with the Orthodox branch of the Society of Friends.

The daughter's religious sympathies were on the side of her mother, to whom she was very closely attached.[2] Emma also had strong conscientious scruples against worldly amusements such as

---

[a]Elias Hicks (19 March 1748 - 27 February 1830) was a Friends minister from Long Island, New York. By "unitarian teaching," Malone means Hicks's dispute with Orthodox Friends over the Trinity, the authority of Scripture, and Christ's death as an atonement for sin - all of which Hicks was reported to have denied. In 1828 Malone's grandparents, Levi and Mary Bye Pennington, met Hicks at New Garden, Ohio, and at Ohio Yearly Meeting, and sided with the Orthodox Friends.

[b]Charles Brown operated a livery stable at 263 Detroit Street in 1874, and owned a grocery store at 351 Bridge Street from 1875-1884. In 1884 they moved to the north side of Franklin Avenue across from Pennington Street (named by Hezekiah Malone for Mary Ann). For data on the Brown family, see endnote 2.

dancing, theater going, and card-playing, and she participated in none of them.

Margaret Haight Brown[3]

A few winters before our Quaker revival under the leadership of Nathan and Esther Frame, Emma Brown had regularly attended a gracious revival that was conducted by Mr. D. L. Moody[4] in the autumn of 1879.[c] She had assented to most of his preaching, but when Mr. Moody gave an opportunity for a decision for Christ as Saviour from sin, she could not, or would not do so. She always said she that was so biased by her father and grandfather's arguments against Jesus being God that she was unable to bring herself to pray in His name for forgiveness.

Nevertheless, her spiritual convictions kept her in the meeting every night. But this last night had now come, and the last call had been given to stand before the great congregation to take Christ as

---

[c]Emma (Brown) Malone (30 January 1859 - 12 May 1924) was twenty years old in the fall of 1879. She was a graduate of West High School in Cleveland, where she had been the valedictorian.

her Saviour, and finally she made the decision. She stood to her feet. She tarried in the after meeting where further instructions and prayer were made for those deciding, but she could not pray in the name of Jesus.

Following the meeting, Emma went home, but not to sleep. She had to settle it. She cried and wept and prayed, but not in His name. This continued for hours until fairly exhausted she broke out in words and said, "Well, Lord, if I must, I will, I do. I ask for forgiveness in the name of Jesus Christ." With that surrender and that prayer for forgiveness in the name and for the sake of Jesus Christ, there came a witness of the Spirit for her forgiveness and the incoming of light that never left a doubt in her heart, and she began to sing the dear old song, "Hallelujah, 'tis done. I believe on the Son. I'm saved by the blood of the crucified One." She then went to sleep saying these words, and awoke the next morning still singing in her heart "Tis done." Later her mother told her that all day she knew what had happened by her song and lighted face and joyful spirit, and all the rest of her life she bore the light that came in that night when she prayed in the name of Jesus, and all her friends will testify that the light could be seen in her face and even in her photograph, as is proved by a Chinese woman who saw her photograph for the first time in the missionary's [Emily Moore][d] room.[5] [The incident with the photograph was reported as follows by the missionary]:

> You remember when Moses went up into the mountain in the midst of the cloud of glory . . . and when he came down his face shone so that he had to put a veil over his face. I often think of that when I think of Mrs. Malone and her shining face.
> One morning a Chinese woman who was helping us in the home . . . . . stood before that picture [of Walter and Emma Malone] silently weeping. I said, "Why, what is the matter?" and she said, "Tell me about the people in this picture." I said, "Why do you want to know?" She replied, "The face of that woman is like the face of Jesus. I know she must be a child of God. I want you to tell me about her."
> As I told her about her, she said, "I believe that woman would love me. I am so glad to see even her picture."[6]

---

[d]Emily M. Moore (25 June 1895 - 16 August 1989) was a minister, a missionary to China (1919-1923), and a teacher at Cleveland Bible College (1937-1957).

Emma's testimonies in the Friends meeting were always short, simple, and sweet. Finally on one Sabbath I asked her to lead the Young People's meeting on the next Sabbath afternoon. She agreed, but in the mid-week she wrote me to say that she did not see how she could assume such a great responsibility as leading a meeting, but she added that if I would not excuse her I would just have to pray for her and she would try to do her best. She then led her first public meeting, and of course she did so beautifully in the Spirit. Thus Emma and I were brought out as the first-fruits (or signs) of Cleveland Bible Institute. For in this way there were brought into the ministry scores of young people by opening the way for them to exercise themselves in the ministry by having them gain experience in leading meetings and leading others to Christ.

It was in this way, side by side, that Emma and I began our ministry. Neither of us could tell just when we began to preach. But as "the spirit of testimony is the spirit of prophecy," so we began to preach.

The next thing to decide was what to do about someone to preach when Nathan and Esther Frame closed their meetings, for we had the meeting house well filled with people, to say the least, who were interested if not under real conviction for sin or holiness of heart. After a little consultation, we called a meeting of the concerned Friends to see what the next step should be, as Nathan and Esther Frame had other engagements to which they must go. And to this called meeting I proposed we ask Dr. Dougan Clark[e] of Richmond, Indiana, who was head of the Biblical Department of Earlham College, whom I had heard and learned to love in the Friends meeting in Cincinnati, Ohio.[7] To this suggestion they were all agreed, and we wrote a letter of invitation which he accepted for Sundays for a few weeks, and we all loved to hear him preach and give his fatherly advice.

By this time we all had learned to love him and enjoyed his ministry so much that he was invited to stay a year, which he did. He was known to be a holiness preacher, and under this kind of sermon

---

[e]Dougan Clark (17 May 1828 - 10 October 1896) was the leading theologian in the holiness wing of American Quakerism in the later 19th century. Clark was in Cleveland from the fall of 1882 through the fall of 1883. He provided intellectual underpinnings for the revivalistic evangelical Quakerism introduced to Cleveland Friends by the Frames and carried on by Walter and Emma Malone.

the meeting thrived. Emma Brown and I both came out for the baptism of the Holy Spirit[f] and were sanctified about this time while Dr. Clark was still with us.[8] After he left us, we invited other ministers for a longer or shorter time, or as it seemed best.[9] Our meetings were real revival meetings, and when no visiting minister was present I often did the preaching, but for many years my special care was to see to it that we had someone to do the preaching as well as the pastoral work, for I had all I could do with my stone business and to teach my Sunday School lessons to my teachers' meeting on Saturday night, and get them fired up for the Sunday's lesson, to superintend the Sunday school, stopping as I used to in this class or that when I detected a weakness and inability to hold the class, or when the teacher was having trouble with the boys and girls. And then I always had charge of the Young People's revival meeting at 4:00 on Sunday afternoons.

I helped in the morning and evening services, and for a year at a time we had an altar service every Sunday afternoon. Sometimes I would turn the whole Sunday School into an altar service and get young people converted by the score. I once saw as high as fifty converted in that Sunday School in one afternoon.

One thing that helped to develop me as a Bible teacher was my Saturday night Bible class, which was especially for Sunday School teachers, and for the teachers in our school in particular. I spent hours studying my Bible and praying, and when I was especially weary I spent an hour or two in Bible study, which would always refresh me.

Now the cry of my heart was how to keep the crowds of young people growing in grace who were being converted in the Sunday School and Young People's meetings. The Bible reading and Bible study were doing me, as well as others, so much good that we thought that if we could just get others into the habit of regularly reading their Bibles and praying, then we would get them established and make them successful Christian workers.

---

[f]Of his "baptism of the Holy Spirit," Walter Malone wrote,
"Suddenly and blessedly . . . I felt myself in the atmosphere of love, Divine love of melting tenderness, a love not known heretofore; a love for everyone and a longing for every minister and every Christian to receive this fulness of the blessing of the Gospel."
For a more complete account of this "baptism," see endnote 9.

We decided that Emma Brown and her cousin Florence[g] should prepare the Bible selections which to be read each day, and I was responsible to get them printed on sheets that covered every day in the month so that everybody would have one and be sure to read the Bible daily, and to remember while we read the Bible that this was the Word of the Lord. We would remind the students that He talks to us through His Word, and when we pray we talk to Him.

Our motto was "Out and out for Christ." We were not ashamed of being known as Christians, and of talking to our friends and chums and trying to get them to become Christians. It can easily be seen how out of this little beginning the call of the Lord to open the Bible Institute came to us later.

At this time I ushered the congregation to their seats, and then took my seat facing the meeting. I also frequently did the preaching, and always shook hands with all as they went out the door. But sometimes we had no minister. On those occasions, I would go over to the Evangelical Association which was not far distant from the church, where I would invite one of their ministers to come over to preach for us.

Our Sunday School was so large that it was almost impossible to get them into the room and have class at all. We had two classes on the platform, one on either side of the desk, one in the entrance hall, etc. So one summer we decided to rent a roller skating rink which was in the neighborhood for Sunday afternoons for the Sunday School and the Young People's meeting while we enlarged the meeting house, which we did and the Lord greatly blessed our Sunday School. However, on the day when the enlarging of the meeting house was finished and when we brought the Sunday School back into it, we found that the trouble of enlarging it was little help, for the room was just as crowded as it was before. Over five hundred scholars were enrolled.

These were the conditions in the Quaker meeting when Emma Brown and I were married on January 19, 1886. The people who gathered for our wedding were a very mixed or cosmopolitan company. We invited our friends and acquaintances without any

---

[g]Florence Brown was a Cleveland artist who painted the portrait of Mary Ann Malone in chapter 1. Brown was confined to a wheelchair, yet despite her disability she later went to Wisconsin as a pastor and evangelist where she traveled about in a "gospel wagon" that was built to accommodate her wheelchair.

respect of persons, so there were present in the meeting house three or four judges of the city, two or three lawyers, several doctors, some preachers, and also among the number of those who gathered were two or three wonderful colored women who were Godly saintly Christians.

After Dr. Clark left our meeting, we invited different ministers to speak and spend more or less time with us as the way opened. Nathan and Esther Frame spent much of two years with us. John T. Dorland was a great blessing to our meeting and strengthened it.[h]

---

[h]John T. Dorland was a respected Canadian Friend. Dorland came to Cleveland in January 1886 to attend the wedding of Walter and Emma Malone, and remained until "the end of the year 1887." In Cleveland, he spent the two "best and most privileged [years] of my life." Dorland considered Euclid Avenue to be "unsurpassed as a residential street by any I have ever seen," and spoke of "excursions into dark territories" - which appears to be a reference to Cleveland's slums where mission work was conducted by the Malones. He described the Friends Meeting as a place where "a very few old and wealthy families" worship with "a number of . . young families, and a number of poor." To Dorland, the poor were "a blessing." See William King Baker, *John T. Dorland* (London: Headley, 1898), pp. 55-61. For more material on Dorland, see the Dorland Friends Collection at Pickering College in New Market, Ontario.

ENDNOTES

[1]The Browns were Hicksite Friends, and members of the Yonge Street Meeting. Emma Malone's father, Charles W. Brown (8 March 1835 - 9 January 1919), was a son of Ira Brown (17 April 1802 - 4 December 1886) and Mercy Elizabeth (Widdifield) Brown (1 October 1805 - 6 May 1857), and a grandson of Abraham (b. 1757/58) and Catherine Brown, who migrated from Rhode Island to Ferrisburgh in Addison County, Vermont,and from there to Canada. Ira's older brother, Nicholas Brown (b. 1788), provoked the Orthodox-Hicksite split in New York Yearly Meeting when he proposed replacing the Orthodox clerk with a Hicksite. See H. Larry Ingle, *Quakers in Conflict: The Hicksite Reformation* (Knoxville: University of Tennessee, 1986), p. 232. For the Hicksite background of Emma (Brown) Malone, see Martha P. Grundy, "The Quaker Background of Emma Brown Malone," in David Johns, ed., *Hope and a Future: Three Evangelical Friends,* pp. 19-47. For materials on the Haight and Brown family genealogies, I am indebted to Nancy P. Speers of Swarthmore College, Philadelphia; Jane V. Zavitz of Pickering College, New Market, Canada; and William E. Britnell.

[2]The Haights were generally Orthodox Friends, and pioneers in the Quaker settlement at Pickering. Margaret (Haight) Brown, a daughter of Allen and Sarah Haight, was married to Charles W. Brown in 1858 by a Wesleyan Methodist minister. Margaret's mother - who was also Emma Malone's grandmother - was a Quaker minister who undertook missionary journeys in a one-horse wagon with no springs, sitting on straw or pine branches to cushion her ride.

[3]I am indebted to Malcolm Malone, an adopted son of J. Walter Malone, Jr., for this picture of Margaret (Haight) Brown.

[4]Dwight Lyman Moody (1837-1899) was the leading American evangelist in the later nineteenth century. Moody shared with the Malones a dislike for theological controversy, "worldly amusements" and "greedy" businessmen, and a commitment to "soul-winning," "holiness," Christian education, pacifism (Moody had been a conscientious objector during the Civil War), and premillennialism. Moody's messages were characterized - in George Marsden's phrase - by "sentiment" rather than sensation." See George Marsden, *Fundamentalism and American Culture. The Shaping of Twentieth-Century Evangelicalism: 1870-1925* (Oxford: Oxford University, 1980), p. 32.

[5]Malone's notes at this point in his manuscript read "The Story of Her Photograph in China," which means that he intended to insert this story at this point. In compliance with Walter's wishes, I have inserted the following story from a letter from Emily Moore (a Quaker missionary to China) to Walter Malone after the death of Emma in 1924.

[6]Byron L. Osborne, *The Malone Story: The Dream of Two Quaker Young People* (Newton, Kansas, United Printing, 1970), p. 17.

[7]Dougan Clark was the grandson of Nathan Hunt, the leader of North Carolina Yearly Meeting in the first half of the 19th century. Clark attended Friends Boarding School (now Guilford College) in North Carolina and Friends Boarding School in Rhode Island (now Moses Brown School). He received a medical degree from the University of Pennsylvania in 1861, gave up medicine in 1866 to teach Greek and Latin at Earlham. In 1870 he resumed the practice of medicine, but later returned to Earlham to establish a Biblical Department.

As a teacher, Clark was praised by a student at Earlham for bringing to life "all the poetry of the poets, all the philosophy of life in the historians, all the eloquence in the orators. "See Richard Eugene Wood, "Evangelical Quakers in the Mississippi Valley, 1854-1894, (Ph.D. diss., University of Minnesota, 1985), p. 164.

For Clark's influence on Walter and Emma Malone, see Thomas Hamm, "The Quaker Tradition of Young Walter Malone," in *Hope and A Future*, pp. 1-18.

[8]See Osborne, pp. 19-20. Osborne quotes from an article in the *Evangelical Friend* (2 June 1910) in which Malone described this experience as follows:

> For many months past, there had been a deep hunger in my heart that words could not express, a longing for an anointing with fresh oil. I wanted what George Fox received that made him different from other preachers of his day and generation. As expressed in his [Fox's] own words, "I knew Jesus and He was very precious to my soul, but I found something in me that would not keep patient and kind. I did what I could to keep it down, but it was there. I besought Jesus to do something for me, and when I gave Him my will, He came into my heart and cast out all that would not be sweet, all that would not be kind, all that would not be patient, and then He shut the door." Or as Rufus Jones puts in in his *Life of George Fox* (page 226), speaking of the priests, Fox said, "they pleaded for imperfection and to sin as long as they lived, but did not like to hear of Christ teaching His people Himself, and making people as clean while on earth, as Adam and Eve were before they fell."
>
> I found through His Spirit, that I was not as gentle and kind and tender as He wanted me to be, that I was not as longsuffering, and that I did not always love my brethren with the love of the Master; being sometimes critical and harsh. Oh the hunger and travail of my soul for a baptism of love and power and pain, real birth pain, that would bring souls into the Kingdom! So I prayed and cried, until one day, while pleading with Him over II Peter 1:4, for the fulfillment of the exceeding great and precious promises which are given to us, by which we are made partakers of the Divine nature, suddenly and blessedly, He fulfilled the promise to me, and I felt myself in the atmosphere of love, Divine love of melting tenderness, a love not known heretofore; a love for everyone and a longing for every minister and every Christian to receive this fullness of the blessing of the Gospel.

Malone's "baptism" is similar to Moody's experience in 1871, which was such that Moody "had to ask God to withhold His hand, lest he die on the very spot for joy." See Marsden, p. 78. It may also have been similar to "a definite experience of sanctification and the renewing of the Holy Ghost" that was experienced by David Tatum in 1864 under the preaching of the Methodist evangelist Phoebe Palmer. See the *Evangelical Friend*, Vol. 8 (25 October 1912), p. 7.

[9]The principal visiting ministers from 1882-1885 were Esther and Nathan Frame (one and a half years, with Nathan away for much of this time), Dougan Clark (one year), and Caroline Talbot (four or five months). In short, during two of the three years the principal visiting minister was a woman.

Chapter Five

VISION OF THE DRAGON

Sketch by Barbara Drennan[1]

"This vision has always given me courage. . . ."

A little time after we were married [on 19 January 1886], I had my first breakdown in health, for I had never been very strong physically in my life.[2] And now I was attending to the stone business every day, and was often compelled to make hurried trips to New York, Philadelphia, Washington, D.C., St. Louis, and Chicago, sometimes going by night and returning the next night, besides my church work.

By this time the business was growing nicely, and I remember one day how a feeling of relaxation came over me and my spirit. I remember saying to myself, "Well, business has gotten to the point where I will not need to pray and intercede so much, and now I can take things a little easier." But at once the Spirit of the Lord said, "My child, from this time on all the health thee has thee will get from me in answer to prayer."

The Dragon

I cannot tell whether it was then, or perhaps a little later, but it must have been that night during my evening devotions that I seemed to have a vision,[3] for suddenly I was walking along a narrow path under an overhanging cliff, with a great chasm yawning at my feet. On my left it was very deep and dark, and I could see nothing but clouds as it were of smoke. On my right hand stood the high overhanging cliff that covered my path entirely, so that I could neither turn to the right hand nor to the left. And just in front of me was the terrible dragon with a terrible mouth open, showing terrible teeth. It had terrible feet with powerful wings which had on them long sharp claws that he raised to strike me down. Yet each time that he raised his black pinions to strike me, I would just say, "Jesus, Jesus" and take a step forward, and his dragon wings would fall short of me.[a]

It was in this vision that I saw what faced and opposed me, and I realized that my only safety lay in the name of Jesus. I saw what was to oppose me henceforth, and I saw what was my only way of progress. I have gone forward ever since in that precious name. In sickness and in health I saw what the result would be if I should relax. My only safety lay in going forward. I knew better than to relax or to fear the arch-fiend of the pit when I saw him ready to devour me. A text from James says - "Resist the devil and he will flee from you" - and a text from Peter - "Be sober, be vigilant; because your adversary the devil, as a roaring lion, walketh about, seeking whom he may devour."

---

[a]Visions are more common in Quaker, Catholic, and Eastern Orthodox history than in mainstream Protestantism. Well-known Quaker visionaries include George Fox, who reported seeing an "Ocean of Light" and an "Ocean of Darkness," and Joseph Hogue, who saw a vision that led him to foretell the American Civil War. David Tatum, a Quaker minister who appears to have helped persuade Walter Malone to attend the Friends meeting in Cleveland, received a "definite experience of sanctification and the renewing of the Holy Ghost" in 1864 under the ministry of Phoebe Worrall Palmer (1807-1867) of New York, an advocate of Holiness or "complete surrender to God." See endnote 3 for an account of Tatum's vision of "the Lord or an angel from heaven."

This vision has always given me courage to know that through the name of Jesus I was more than a conqueror, and that I was more than a match for the enemy. I understood that he could neither crowd me into the great gulf, nor against the walls, nor could all of his infernal power keep me from going forward. He must step backward every time I step forward. Ever since I have known what it meant when the Lord sent me to go and pray for the sick, the demon oppressed or possessed, the afflicted, or the sinner, to lay my hands on them and to pray over them in the name of Jesus.

Demons[b]

Another time when we were praying for the sick, my wife and I were led to lay our hands on this afflicted one, rebuke the demons, and bid them to come out. The Lord opened my eyes to see the demons, and the impression is with me still as clearly as it was on that day. I can still see the angry creature showing his teeth and fiery eyes and growling at us.

One other time, wife[c] and I were called by a saint to pray for her affliction, which was a peculiar one, and she considered it to be an attack of the devil. When we laid our hands upon her and prayed, my wife was given the prayer of faith for her, and she was led to command the demon to come out. She saw the demon depart and so did the afflicted woman who was healed from that hour. These experiences opened our spiritual eyes to see unseen things, and they gave us courage in prayer, for after this we knew what was opposing us.

---

[b]The following two paragraphs were included in Walter Malone's handwritten manuscript, but crossed out in the typed manuscript with the word "omit" written in pencil. I include these paragraphs because I think they help to underscore three components of the faith of Walter Malone: to him, evil was literally Satanic and demonic, no one was immune from its power, and these direct confrontations with this terrifying evil produced in him, not paralyzing fear, but courage.

[c]Walter Malone sometimes refers to Emma Malone as simply "wife," omitting - as in standard English - the word "my."

ENDNOTES

[1]Barbara Drennan is an Instructor of Art at Malone College.

[2]Walter Malone was a patient at the Clifton Springs Sanitarium at Clifton Springs, New York, in May 1887. In a letter to Emma dated 14 May 1887, he wrote,

> If I had not had so many visions of future work and so many assurances, so many promises, I should never expect to get well. . . . Why, I can't walk more than two blocks without my legs paining me, and my head too.

Clifton Springs was a resort where Christians went for rest and healing. The board of the sanitarium included bishops of the Methodist and Episcopal churches and six secretaries of missionary societies. No records survive from 1887.

Byron Osborne told me that Malone's physical problems were exacerbated by exhaustion from overwork, which sometimes forced him to go to bed for several days, where Emma nursed him - Osborne remembers - with "great tenderness, love, and care." At other times, the Malones vacationed in Dunedin, Florida, where five of Walter's brothers owned elegant homes along the Gulf of Mexico: H.P. and C.O. Malone (the two oldest brothers) shared a home at 827 Victoria Drive, L.H. Malone (who Walter and Emma generally visited) lived at 905 Victoria, and J.S. and E.T. Malone at 951 Victoria. For the Malones in Dunedin see William L. Davidson, *Dunedin Through the years: 1850-1978* (Charlotte: Delmar, 1978), pp. 29-30, 33, 61-63, 167-168, 196, 208-209. I am indebted to Vivian Skinner Grant for help with historical data on Dunedin, which is claimed to be the oldest town (1870) on the West Coast of Florida south of Cedar Key. The town's bears the Gaelic name for Edinburgh ("peaceful rest"). So it was to the Malones.

[3]David Tatum, an older minister in the Cleveland meeting when Malone first came to Cleveland, reported that as a younger man he had had a "dream" or "vision" that came to him "many nights in succession" in which he found himself bound with chains and dragged by a "great force toward a lake of flaming fire." Each time that he approached the edge of the lake Tatum "screamed with horror" and awoke from his dream. I do not know if Walter Malone had heard this story. See the *Autobiography of David Tatum: The Formative Years,* pp. 2-3. Tatum also reported "a very remarkable experience" that happened to him in 1860:

> When sitting in a room alone and quiet there suddenly appeared in my presence, and standing before me, a person most graceful in appearance, whose dignity and brightness impressed me with the belief that it was the Lord or an angel from heaven. I was filled with wonder and admiration at the brightness of His appearance and the grandeur of His person, when He addressed me thus: "David, if thou wilt shun temptation and give thyself up to the Lord, and to the service of Christ, God will clothe thee with His armor, and many shall be gathered under thy ministry." When these words were spoken he was suddenly enveloped in a bright shining light, which

emanated from His own person, a glorious brilliancy which no man can describe.

I felt I could not remain in His presence and behold His majesty and glory and live, and I cried aloud, "Oh Lord, have mercy and save me," when suddenly He vanished from my sight and I was left alone, but with an overflowing fullness of the Holy Spirit as never before. And that gentle overflowing continued of great solemnity, and I walked softly as before the Lord, the very ground seemed holy.

See the *Evangelical Friend*, Vol. 8 (25 October 1912), p. 7. Phoebe Palmer, who exerted a profound influence on David Tatum, is called by Mark Noll "one of the most influential Protestant teachers of any kind during the nineteenth century in both the United States and Canada." See Mark A. Noll, *A History of Christianity in the United States and Canada* (Grand Rapids, Michigan: Eerdmans, 1992), p. 182. Palmer's "deeper experience" of Holiness, which occurred on 26 July 1837, followed after the deaths of her three young children.

Students and Faculty at the Training School, 1892-1893

Chapter Six

THE CALL TO BEGIN THE BIBLE INSTITUTE

"The action of the student body embarrassed us greatly. . . ."

Five or six years after we were married, we found our hearts turned to the Lord repeatedly for the young people of the church and at large who had the call of the Lord on their hearts to preach, but for whom there was no way open[a] for the exercise of their gifts. We discovered that the local young people who taught Bible classes and led young people's meetings, cottage meetings, and prayer meetings were developing into Christian workers who gave promise for becoming preachers and missionaries.

The Spirit therefore impressed it on our hearts to open a small school [in Cleveland] in which the Bible could be taught every day, and supervision given to prepare our students to do practical Christian work such as visiting the sick, calling in homes, and personal evangelism. Our thought was to teach the Bible in the mornings, and to leave at least a part of the afternoons and evenings free for home mission work along the lines of home visitation and evangelistic services. Indeed, we wanted to include only those activities that would serve to prepare the individual in a practical way for the service of the Lord.

About that time we discovered that higher criticism[b] and other

---

[a]Phrases like "no way open" or "the way does not seem open" were colloquialisms used by Quakers to say "no."

[b]Late nineteenth century "higher critics," using rationalism, historicism, and natural causation to explain the Bible, tended to be skeptical of supernaturalism, and optimistic about the inherent goodness of humankind - especially "educated," "enlightened," or "civilized" western humankind. For Biblical "higher criticism," religious "modernism," and responses by Benjamin Trueblood and Walter Malone, see endnote 1.

destructive teachings were fast getting a foothold in our denominational colleges.[1] The longer we thought and talked and prayed about
it, the heavier the burden grew to open a small school, and the more
real became the call.

Neither of us had ever visited or seen a Bible Institute. The one
founded by Mr. [Dwight L.] Moody and a small one for girls conducted by Lucy Ryder Meyer in Chicago were the only ones in this country
or in the world so far as we knew.[2] It therefore seemed like assuming
a vast responsibility to attempt to found a Bible Institute. And this was
particularly the case in view of the fact that there was no organization
behind us to share the burden. Moreover, neither my wife nor myself
was reputed as having much ability as Bible teachers. In fact, neither
of us planned to teach unless perchance it might be some minor
subject. We thought our responsibility would be administrative and
menial. It was our hope that we could get Dr. Dougan Clark[c] to come
and teach the Bible and possibly other subjects.

Chicago

About this time a few prominent Friends ministers conferred
and made plans to open a Friends' Theological Seminary very much
after the plan we felt the Lord had given us.[3] They attempted to get
a few Yearly Meetings of Friends to back the undertaking and
co-operate in organizing and managing it. Therefore we saw if that
venture went through successfully there would be no place or need for
the institution we felt on our hearts to open.

This was in the year of the World's Fair in Chicago, and
[William S. Wooten] one of those four or five principal Friends had
bought a large hotel and equipped it to be the Friends' headquarters
during the Fair.[4] They planned at the close of the fair to utilize this
hotel to house the new theological seminary.

I was in Chicago about the first of December 1891, where I
found one of those ministers conducting the noon hour prayer meeting
at the Y.M.C.A., another of them speaking in a popular meeting, the
third [John Henry Douglas] conducting a large Bible Class, and the

---

[c]For Dougan Clark see chapter four.

fourth [Calvin Pritchard] editing a Christian paper[d][the *Christian Worker*].[5] All of them were in popular favor. And what was my surprise when I called at their office one day for a friendly visit to have them invite me into their private office for a conference. They asked me to join forces and unite with them in their plans. They even suggested that I move to Chicago and take the presidency of the Seminary. To these suggestions I replied that I would think it over, talk with my wife, pray over it, see the mind of the Lord regarding it, and let them know.

After reaching home the next day I laid the matter before my wife, and after weeping and praying together, my wife stated that she saw no light in that direction. I went to my "closet" on the third floor, shut the door, and told the Lord that I must know what to do. And as I wept and prayed in the Spirit, He spoke and made it very definite to me that my wife and I were to go forward and open [in Cleveland] the Training School, as we then called it. It was made plain that we would have opposition, and that our authority and right to do this would be questioned. But we had the word of the King behind it and there was to be "no discharge" in that war. It was the "King's Command." "Where the word of the King is, there is power"[6] [Ecclesiastes 8:4].[e] Then He said that those ministers in Chicago were to be "forgotten in the city where they had so done."

The Spirit spoke to me through Ecclesiastes 8 and other portions of Scripture, and gave directions and words to my heart. When I went down to tell my wife the message that the Lord gave me, I found, in the meantime, that she had been shown a vision of the Seminary Company in Chicago that was similar to the revelation to the prophet Jonah under the withered gourd vine. This was December 4th, 1891. Thus we were cut off from having men of note and influence with us, and it was only a few months later that all these

---

[d]In 1891 the *Christian Worker* was owned by three Malone brothers (Walter, Edwin, and William), and had the largest circulation of any Quaker periodical in the United States. In 1894 Walter Malone merged the *Christian Worker* with the *Friends Review* to found the *American Friend*, which - under the editorship of Rufus Jones of Haverford College - became the principal organ for Quakerism in the United States and Canada.

[e]The complete verse reads, "Where the word of a king is, there is power: and who may say unto him, What doest thou?"

men had left Chicago and were "forgotten in the city where they had so done." From that hour of December 4th, 1891 there was but a forward march.

Cleveland

Dr. Dugan Clark, whom we planned would take the head of the work, decided he could not come and help us at all. But we went on, nothing daunted.

Accordingly we rented a vacant house on what is now known as Carnegie Avenue,[7] near to Thirtieth Street, and we advertised the date of opening as March 17th, 1892, although we had neither teachers or matron assured. Both however were promised by the day of the opening. The teacher was a Godly woman, Mrs. Lida [Gressell] Romick [an evangelist and mission worker from Alum Creek, Ohio].[8] Mrs. Romick's associate was Sarah Osmond [from Newberg, Oregon]. Eli Rees also was present, and he tarried for awhile to teach.[9] Mrs. Herrington, the cultured and beautifully mannered saint, came as the matron.[f]

As the day for opening drew near, we felt so incapable that we prayed and asked the Lord not to send more than a half dozen students to start with. Remarkably enough when the day closed just six had registered.[10] But as I recall, there were some thirty or forty in attendance during the first term.[g]

Great days were those. It took courage, especially on the part of my dear wife who had four children to care for, the youngest only four months old. But she was always a General. Both of us did some

---

[f]I have not been able to identify Mrs. Herrington. In addition, Sarah L. Andrews, the principal of the Cleveland Academy (a private school for children from Cleveland's urban aristocracy), also taught during the first year. Andrews worked with Anna A. Thompson in a Faith Rest mission for women at 196 Huntington Street. See the *Cleveland Plain Dealer*, 8 September 1892, p. 3.

[g]If by "first term" Malone means the first academic year, he understates the enrollment. The Register for the first academic year lists the names of fifty six students who took classes at the school: fifteen of these registered for the first session, twenty-seven for the second, twenty-six for the third, and twenty-five for the fourth. However, this list is not complete: for example, Martilla Cox, who enrolled as a student after giving up her classes, is not listed in the Register.

teaching, but I had the [stone] business to attend to while Mrs. Malone had to give much time to home cares.

When Dr. Clark wrote us that he could not come, he recommended a teacher [Martilla - or as she was also known -"Tilly" Cox] who was one of his former students and a graduate of the Bible Department [at Earlham College]. She proved to be a good teacher "about the Bible," but not so good at teaching the Bible itself. It was not long before a committee from the student body waited upon us, saying that if we were going to have this teacher teach, and not teach them ourselves, that they were going home, for it was for our teaching that they had come.

This was a very great surprise to us, and I do not know what else would have caused us to step out and take a prominent place in teaching the Bible. The action of the student body embarrassed us greatly, but the teacher took the news very sweetly, saying she saw that her teaching was not the kind wanted, but if we would allow her, she would stay and enter as a student, taking the regular work, which she did.[h] Thus Mrs. Malone took up the teaching of the Old Testament, and I the teaching of the New.[i]

---

[h]Martilla ("Tilly") Cox, after receiving training in urban mission work in Cleveland, became a pastor and evangelist in Indiana in the Society of Friends.

[i]Emma and Walter Malone served as co-principals. At least fourteen women (Minnie F. Bassett, Esther E. Baird, Florence E. Brown, Martilla Cox, Lizzie M. Dennis [later Leggett], Esther J. Emery, Delia Fistler, Estella Hammond, Belle Harrington [later Babcock], Emma B. Malone, Mary Emily Moore, Susie Norris [later Fitkin], Mary Emily Soule [later Ellison], and Ida A. Ryan) and eleven men (Willis R. Cook, Edgar P. Ellyson, Jermaine B. Emery, Leroy J. Hopper, Willis R. Hotchkiss, Frank M. Hurley, Edwin Jay Lord, Howard Moore, Joseph H. Peele, Leverett J. Rugg, and Fred E. Smith) from the school's first year were recorded as Friends ministers. Esther Baird and Delia Fistler went to India, and Esther Emery to Brazil. Jermain Emery went to Brazil, and Willis Hotchkiss to Kenya.

I know of no other institution in the United States in the 1890's that produced as many women ministers as did this evangelical Quaker school in Cleveland. Readers from liturgical traditions may be interested to note that while Quaker ministers exercised pastoral and prophetic (teaching) functions, they were not permitted - at least in the nineteenth century - to act in a sacerdotal manner, i.e. to baptize, perform marriages (Quaker couples exchanged wedding vows in front of witnesses), or celebrate the eucharist. Walter Malone's friend, Dougan Clark, was fired from Earlham College in 1894 after scandalizing some Friends by being baptized in front of the Ohio Yearly Meeting.

ENDNOTES

[1]Given Malone's faith in his mother's "supernatural" experiences, his own and his wife's visions, his growing indoctrination in "Holiness" theology, he was not predisposed to be receptive to faith of "higher critics" in rationalism, historicism, and natural causation. Given his experiences in the slums of Cleveland and his distrust of "rich men," he was equally predisposed to reject the optimism of the higher critics about the "goodness" of human nature and their triumphalistic views about modern scholarship and American culture. For Malone's response to higher critics who called Old Testament characters "as fabulous as Promethius" and claimed that "the inerrancy and the infallibility of the Bible are no longer possible of belief among reasoning men," see J. Walter Malone, "George Adam Smith and Dr. Cadman at Northfield," *The American Friend*, Vol. 6 (Tenth Month 1899), pp. 946-947. Malone, who regarded higher criticism as an "infidel doctrine," agreed with D.L. Moody, who had said that preachers who accept higher criticism are "doing the devil's work."

For a different view of higher criticism see Benjamin F. Trueblood, "Biblical Criticism - II," *The American Friend*, Vol. 8, (Eighth Month 1901), pp. 725-727. To Trueblood, Christians "must cordially accept its [higher criticism's] service if we are intelligently to maintain our Christian positions before the world." Trueblood was a past president of Penn College in Iowa, and the prime mover behind the attempt to establish a Quaker seminary in Chicago in 1892-1893 with Walter Malone at its head. Malone's refusal was what Arthur Roberts calls "an important turning point in Quaker history." Given their profound disagreement over higher criticism and Malone's lack of university or seminary training, we can indeed wonder what would have happened to Malone - if not to evangelical Quakerism itself - had he felt "led" to the post in Chicago, where he would have encountered two militant forces: the "orthodoxy" - which later became fundamentalism - of Moody Bible Institute and the "modernism" of the Divinity School at the University of Chicago.

[2]In 1885 Lucy Ryder Meyer founded a Training School for City, Home and Foreign missionaries in Chicago. Esther Tuttle Pritchard, a Quaker leader and a friend of the Malones, taught for Mrs. Meyer at this school in the early 1890's. See Mary A. Hill, "The Chicago Training School," *Christian Worker*, Vol. 21 (Twelfth Month 24, 1891), p. 820. Meyer's students, like those of the Malones, did evangelistic work, offered medical help, and went "down into the slums . . . to relieve squalid wretchedness 'for Jesus's sake.'" See Esther Tuttle Pritchard, "A Red Letter Hour," *Christian Worker*, Vol. 22 (Third Month 24, 1892), pp. 178-179.

[3]These leaders included Benjamin Trueblood, former president of Penn College and soon-to-be president of the American Peace Association; John Henry Douglas, a leading evangelist and Walter Malone's neighbor in New Vienna; Calvin Pritchard, editor of the *Christian Worker* and husband of Esther Tuttle Pritchard; and William and Docia Wooton. The Chicago school was to be located in the Park Home Hotel. See the *Christian Worker*, Vol. 22 (10th Month 20, 1892), p. 662; also *Christian Worker*, Vol. 22 (12th Month 29, 1892), p. 821. The hotel, it was

advertised, could provide housing for two hundred to four hundred guests.

[4]William and Docia Wooton had purchased the Park Home Hotel in Chicago where they expected to house one thousand Friends during the World's Fair in 1892.

[5]See John Oliver, "J. Walter Malone: *The American Friend* and an Evangelical Quaker's Social Agenda," *Quaker History*, Vol. 80 (Fall 1991), pp. 63-84. See also Diana Alten [Peterson], "Rufus Jones and *The American Friend*: A Quest for Unity," *Quaker History*, Vol. 74, (Fall 1985), pp. 41-48.

[6]Malone frequently spoke of God as "the King." "The Word of the King" - a favorite phrase of Walter Malone - was the name of a fifteen-minute radio program produced by Cleveland Bible College and broadcast over a network of radio stations. The program began with one station in the later 1940's, and expanded after 1953. At various times it included WDOK, Cleveland, Ohio; WRFD, Worthington, Ohio; WCMW, Canton, Ohio; WTRX, Bellaire, Ohio; WOHP, Bellefontaine, Ohio; WARU, Peru, Indiana; WOMP Wheeling, West Virginia; WHGR Houghton Lake, Michigan; WABJ, Adrian, Michigan; WAVL, Apollo, Pennsylvania; 4VEH, Port-au-Prince, Haiti; as well as stations in Tecumseh, Michigan, Columbus, Ohio, and central Africa. The program was discontinued in June 1960. Scripts and recordings from the programs are in the Malone College Archives.

[7]The school was located at 133 Sibley (later Carnegie Avenue) from 1892-1894. This rented house may have been torn down a few years later: at least a city plat map for 1898 shows no building on this property which was owned by Sarah K. Todd. In 1895 the Workers' Training School was located at 236 East Prospect (later Carnegie Avenue), in 1896 it was at 277 East Prospect, and in 1897 at 263 Cedar Avenue (with renumbering this later became 3201 Cedar).

[8]For Lida Romick's work as an evangelist in sod houses in Kansas in 1883 see Lida Romick, "Extracts from the Diary of an Evangelist," *Evangelical Friend*, Vol 2 (1906), pp. 390, 407, 440-441, 484-485, 502-503. For her work in the slums of Brooklyn, New York, in 1877, see Edwin B. Bronner, ed., *An English View of American Quakerism: The Journal of Walter Robson (1842-1929) Written During the Fall of 1877, While Traveling among American Friends* (Philadelphia: American Philosophical Society, 1970, pp. 132-133. See also Lida G. Romick, "How Mary Went as a Missionary," *Evangelical Friend*, Vol. 2 (5th Month 10th, 1906), pp. 298-299. Romick later served as the superintendent of giving for Oregon Yearly Meeting. Her death on 6 July 1912 was reported in the *Evangelical Friend*, Vol.8 (18 July 1912), p.14.

[9]Eli Rees, the lone male among the first teachers, fathered a child soon after leaving Cleveland. He confessed his "sin" to Quaker leaders, married the mother of his child, and became a respected leader in the Society of Friends.

[10]The Register lists seven students as enrolling on 17 March 1892. These were Jermain B. Emery, Esther J. Emery, Lizzie M. Dennis, Frank M. Hurley, Alice Hartley, Alonzo R. Markham, and Thomas H. Pitts. The register is in the archives at Malone College.

Chapter Seven

OUR MISSION WORK

The Cleveland Academy of Music[1]

"Many a mother's wandering boy was captured for God and sent home."

Mission at the Music Hall

At that time, we rented the worst theater in the city for our mission work, and as a place where we could train our Cleveland Bible Institute students how to do mission work, and where we could show them how the old gospel was still able to transform men and women by the power of God. This theater was the old Music Hall of Cleveland.[2] The hall was over four saloons, with two saloons on each side of the entrance to the building. It was at this time the worst theater in the city.[a]

We had meetings there each Wednesday and Sunday night, and many were the battles royal we had there. The Salvation Army and other officers often helped,[b] and the singing of students and other young people drew crowds and sent conviction deep.[3]

It was at this sort of a meeting on a Wednesday night, before a crowd of drunkards and all sorts of sinners, that I asked the teacher spoken of above [Martilla Cox] to give a message and preach. She replied, "I have never given a testimony in my life." I said, "I did not ask if you could preach, but to go to the Lord and get a message from Him for these sin-sick souls." Again she answered, "I cannot preach." I said again, "I did not ask you if you could preach. I simply asked you to get a message from the Lord for these sin-sick souls." I had heard her read a beautiful paper at a missionary meeting some time before, and this is what gave me the courage to press this request with her.

A day or two later she came trembling, with a pathos in her voice that she had never had before, and said, "After hours of prayer and tears I have a little message on my heart for those people." I said, "Praise the Lord, we will have it tonight." It was a message from the King to His rebel subjects, and was very effective.

After she had given a few more messages in church, prayer meetings, and other services, there came a call for an evangelist from the superintendent of the Indiana Quarterly Meeting to which she belonged. I wrote to him that I had a good one and sent this young teacher. After two or three weeks of evangelistic meetings she reported that she had had 175 conversions. This is only a sample of how the Cleveland Bible Institute does its work, and what makes our students such successful preachers and soul-winners.

---

[a]The Cleveland Academy of Music stood on Bank Street between Frankfort and St. Clair, and graduated such prominent American actors as Edwin Forrest, Charlotte Cushman, Edwin Booth, and John Wilkes Booth. The theater occupied the third and fourth floors, and seated more than two thousand persons. The auditorium, which was two hundred feet long, eighty feet wide, and twenty-seven feet high, was graced with a great chandelier. For more information, see endnote 2.

[b]Oberlin College students led by the Rev. George D. Wilder in the summer of 1892 held religious meetings on Sunday mornings at the Music Hall. Their purposes appear to be identical with those of the Malones. See endnote 3.

A Fire

We had many glorious and blessed meetings during those months in that old Music Hall, but the four saloons got too discouraged to do anything "while those Quakers are here." They threatened to move unless the owners would move us out, which they decided to do. They gave us notice that the next Sunday night would be the last meeting we could have.

We advertised the closing meeting and had a large crowd. Then, after a sermon and an altar service there came the closing season of prayer, and a special prayer was given for those who had found their Saviour in that old theater. This prayer was led by my dear wife, and what a prayer it was. She thanked the Lord for the months of blessing, for souls saved, for bodies healed, and then she broke through and told the Lord how sorry we were to give up the theater and asked Him to bless the saloon keepers who were forcing us out. Then she added as by the spirit of prophecy, "Lord, we would rather see the building burn to the ground than go back to its old work of wrecking men and women."

The meeting closed, but before morning the building had strangely caught fire, nobody knew how, and burned to the ground.[4] Headlines in the daily paper the next day told the story. It said, among other things, that "the owner should have known better than to have let those Quakers have it, and expect to get it back."

A Fine-Looking Man

One interesting story came as a sequel to one of those Sunday meetings. A year or two later, possibly more, at the close of the after meeting when I was conducting a service at the Y.M.C.A. on a Sabbath afternoon, a fine-looking man, who was finely dressed, pushed his way through the crowd and tarried to shake hands with me, and to say an appreciative word. "Brother Malone," he said, "you don't remember me, do you?" "No," I said, "I don't believe I do." "Well," he replied, "do you remember one Sunday night at the close of the meeting in the old theater when you and your wife tarried with an altar service, and there were two low-down filthy drunkards who would not get down at the altar to pray, and you tarried and prayed with them until they were both converted?" I answered, "Yes, I do remember those two men. They were two of the worst sinners who I ever saw converted." "Well," he said,

> I was one of them. I know I have been saved these two or three years and have my own home again, have my little family with me, and have my little business, and am doing well as a Christian.

I said, "Praise the Lord for that night's work."

Whosoever Will Mission

After the theater burned, we rented the old Free Methodist Church downtown, which was in a good place [a district that one minister called Satan's throne"]ᶜ to catch the "down and outs." We called it "The Whosoever Will Mission." We began by giving a breakfast to the poor, the outcast, the drunkard, and the harlot every Sunday morning. Hundreds came to every one of these morning services, as well as to the other meetings.

We began the breakfast at nine o'clock in the morning, and closed when the last seeker at the altar got through. We gave them all the sandwiches and coffee that they could eat, and then we gave them

---

ᶜThe Whosoever Will Mission, which was also called the Friends Mission Chapel, was located at the corner of Brownell Street and Central Avenue. It served a district that was labeled "Satan's Throne" by the Rev. Dr. H.C. Haydn, pastor of Cleveland's Old Stone (Presbyterian) Church.

In 1892-1893 "Satan's Throne" extended for a radius of half a mile around Public Square, i.e. it was located on the western edge of Cleveland's fashionable Euclid Avenue. Haydn reported that this district contained tenements which were "plague spots" with "bad ventilation, bad sewage, and worse than useless fire escapes," four hundred saloons, most of Cleveland's "gambling resorts" and wholesale liquor stores, 40 houses of prostitution "with perhaps five inmates to a house," and a population of "15,000 that is augmented by many thousands every evening who squander both their money and themselves." See the *Cleveland Plain Dealer*, 30 January 1893, p. 8. For opium "dens" operated by Chinese (the newspaper called them "Mongolians") and by Cleveland's "swell crookdom" on Woodland, St. Clair, Howe, and Central Avenue, see the *Cleveland Plain Dealer*, 27 February 1893, p. 3.

the gospel.[d] We closed with an altar service where many were converted. Many a mother's wandering boy was captured for God and sent
home. Time and again some drunken young man was created anew by
the blood of Jesus and so cleaned up and changed that you would not
know him at the next meeting.[5]

We found our Cleveland Bible Institute students very rapidly
growing in this mission work, making following-up calls, exhorting,
preaching, praying with sinners, and getting them converted. Another
phase of mission work was, we sent students in groups of two or three
to do house-to-house calling, give tracts and extend personal invitations to come to Christian meetings.

We often drew up maps of the district or neighborhood, and
assigned two young people to certain city blocks. This was their parish,
for they were the pastors. They were to call at the homes and conduct
cottage prayer meetings or Bible classes within their parishes each
week. If any were sick, they were to take fruit or other appetizing
dainties, for which wife and I agreed to pay. They always had an
excuse for calling to see if the children were in Sunday School, and do
whatsoever the pastor and preacher should do.

All this work was to be reported at the Institute at personal
work hour. The calling was often made easy by special invitations that
were printed by the church every week or two, which the students took
to each household in their parishes.

---

[d]The Malones provided 10,000 meals at the Whosoever Will Mission to
Cleveland's poor between Christmas 1892 and the spring of 1893. This included a
turkey dinner at Christmas. See endnote 5.

ENDNOTES

[1]The picture of the Cleveland Academy of Music is courtesy of the Cleveland Public Library.

[2]The Cleveland Academy of Music, built in 1852, was called "the most famous theater in the history of Cleveland, and one of the most celebrated in the United States." See Samuel P. Orth, *The History of Cleveland* (Chicago: S.J. Clarke, 1910), p. 438. The *Cleveland Plain Dealer*, 9 September 1892, p.8, reported that Booth "acted there a very few weeks indeed before the assassination of President Lincoln. It is unlikely that he played any engagements afterward." The newspaper asserted that "every actor of note who appeared on the stage between 1856 and 1875" had performed in this theater.

[3]A British Friend who visited Henrietta and Sarah Titus, two women from the Malones' school, who were doing mission work in the slums of Brooklyn, New York, noted that the women were "dressed in ancient Quaker garb and wholly in black." See John W. Graham, "American Papers - V," *The British Friend*, Vol. 6 (2nd Month 1897), p. 33. Walter Malone wrote to Rufus Jones of Haverford College in 1894 to request Jones's help in securing Quaker bonnets from Friends in Philadelphia for women who worked with the poor in Cleveland. See Malone, letter to Rufus Jones, 6 April 1894, in Rufus M. Jones Papers, The Quaker Collection, Haverford College, Haverford, Pa. For Oberlin students at the Music Hall see the *Cleveland Plain Dealer*, 27 August 1892, p. 3. The students planned to undertake "a vast missionary work in the city, branching out in all directions to establish Sunday schools and missions and to visit the needy."

[4]See the *Cleveland Plain Dealer*, 9 September 1892, p. 8. The last service was on Wednesday evening 8 September 1892. The fire, which was ignited by workmen while repairing the building, gutted the theater. The saloons were only slightly damaged.

[5]For the work of feeding the poor at the Whosoever Will Mission see J. Walter Malone, "Annual Report to Yearly Meeting of Evangelistic and Pastoral Committee," *Minutes of the Eighty-First Ohio Yearly Meeting of the Friends Church, Held at Mt. Pleasant, Ohio, 1893* (Columbus, Ohio: Nitschke, 1893), p. 31.

Chapter Eight

MY FIRST TWO FUNERALS

"What is the use of praying for Jim? Even if the Lord should heal him he would just go on in his sinful ways."

One day when I reached home from my business office downtown, I found a carriage waiting for me at the door to take me to see a sick man [Jim] who they feared was dying. He had been suffering all day as well as the night before, and the doctor and nurse were unable to ease the pain and stop the sickness.

I knew him in a business way as a stonecutter. He was well known to be a very Godless man who drank hard, and whose wife was no better than himself, and possibly worse.

There were three families of them living within a square of each other. One was a brother, and the third a brother-in-law, and each home had a child in our Sunday School. None of them attended church anywhere. One little son in each home had been very sick for a day or two, and one of them had died the night before. Just as he was near death's door, this brother was taken terribly sick, so there was sickness in each home, and this made them terribly frightened, especially when this man was taken so sick with no relief of the pain for two days and nights. And they should have been frightened.

When I reached the home, he was suffering intensely. His wife was walking the floor, wringing her hands, crying, almost screaming, with death on their track. When I entered the home and spoke to him, she at once began again to walk the floor and wring her hands, and she cried out, "Oh! Mr. Malone, pray for Jim, pray for Jim!" I asked her, "What is the use of praying for Jim? Even if the Lord should heal him, he would just go on in his sinful ways." "Oh, no," she cried, "he would be a Christian if he got healed.

I asked Jim if he would repent, and through his groans he said that he would. I asked them both if they would pray, and if they would forsake all sin and live for Jesus Christ. They protested that they never had prayed and did not know how, so I told them to just ask God to forgive them for their sins for Jesus' sake.

I led in a simple prayer, and Jim followed sentence by sentence till I was pretty well satisfied with his repentance, but his wife would not pray. She knelt there by the bedside and cried, but she would not pray or even say a prayer after me, but I insisted that I would not pray for Jim until she prayed too. Then, finally in desperation, she followed me in prayer. Then I laid my hand on Jim's head and prayed the prayer of faith, which the Lord says in James 5: 14-15 will raise him up.

The Lord answered, and the pain stopped. Jim turned over in bed with his face to the wall and went to sleep. When he awoke he was well, and was in attendance at the funeral of the little boy the next day which I was to conduct. This was the first funeral in which I was ever in charge.

My very soul went out to that family, and to their connections, especially after the Lord's leading already. I wanted them all to be saved. So after the singing and the message from the Word that the Lord gave me, I called for a time of humiliation, prayer, forsaking of sin, and crying out to God. I had a little altar service on my hands. Nearly everyone of the three families fell on their knees, prayed, and cried. I really think that a definite work was done for eternity.

My sister, Alice M. Terrell,[a] an elder in the church, thought that this was a rather irregular and peculiar kind of funeral, and she took the occasion to tell me that preachers did not have altar services at funerals, and that she had never seen one before. I told her she would have to excuse me this time as I did not know any better, and as they were all sinners and about to die, I wanted them to get saved.

In the meantime, the other boy died in the other family. We had a large funeral, and I had another altar service with the men of three generations at the altar together. The children, the parents, and

---

[a]Alice Malone Terrell, the widow of Dr. Pleasant Terrell, was state superintendent of Sunday School work for the Woman's Christian Temperance Union in Ohio in 1889 and chair of the entertainment committee for the National W.C.T.U. Convention. See the *Union Signal*, 6 "September 1894, p. 10. See also the *Union Signal*, 17 October 1889, and the *National Minutes* of the W.C.T.U., 1889, p. cxcvi.

grandparents all prayed and cried together for mercy, and I told my sister that I did not know any better again than to have an altar service, that they never went to church, and they would not know that it was not according to polite society.

These were my first two funeral services.

J. Walter Malone

Chapter Nine

THE SPIRIT WORKING IN THE FAMILY CIRCLE

"this sickness was not for us, but for a testimony to others."

The Children

Although we had many attacks of sickness, it was our custom to thoroughly search the camp to see if it were not a call to a deeper heart life along some line, and a call to prayer. We hardly knew what it was to have a doctor in our family, except when the little ones came to our home.

When sickness came to the family, we would accept it, and take the occasion as a call from God to come and see Him. Then we would have careful searchings of heart, and prayers, and many times confessions would be made to each other. This plan worked well with the children, and with those assisting us in the home whom we regularly asked into family worship, and some of them were converted. We always felt that these times of sickness and afflictions were chastenings of the Lord, a call to humble ourselves under the hand of God, to be exercised thereby, and to bear the peaceful fruits of righteousness. We came out "more than conquerors through Him who loved us."

We had many close calls in the family when the life of the sick one was despaired of by the doctor. It seemed at times that we had received them from the dead. Carroll [Brown Malone],[1] our eldest son,[a] went so low on one occasion that he looked up into my eyes and

---

[a]Carroll Brown Malone later taught physics at Tsinghia College, Peking, China, and history at Oberlin College, Miami University (Ohio), Colorado College (Colorado Springs, Colorado), and Tunghai University (Taichung, Taiwan). For further data, see endnote 1.

said, "Papa, I see the beautiful city." Later that day the Lord revealed to us the trouble, and showed us what to do for him. Of course we did it, and he was healed at once.

[J.] Walter [Malone, Jr.],[2] our second son,[b] became so sick that he bade me good-by at the midnight hour. I told him, "My darling, you cannot go." I called his mother, and we united again in prayer and were heard as we pressed our case to His heart of love. This boy too was healed. "Many are the afflictions of the righteous, but the Lord delivereth him out of them all."

Esther,[c] our eldest daughter, was a child of severe and oft afflictions.[3] We felt she was given to us by the Lord in answer to prayer, and it took prayer to keep her. One of her illnesses occurred on the day after our son Walter was well enough to be out after recovering from a serious case of pneumonia in which he had been cared for night and day for months by a doctor and nurse and had had a very close call with death. It was after this doctor and nurse had been dismissed that Esther was taken sick with double pneumonia.

The morning after she was taken ill she was very much worse. But we prayed over her and felt that we had the Word of the Lord, and that it was very definite. It was that she was too sick for a doctor to reach the case. If we got a doctor, she would die. But if we would rest the case with Him, He would heal her. This we knew would bring criticism from our friends, but we believed it would bring the blessing from the Lord. So of course we decided to obey His word.

I went to my business late the next morning with a very heavy heart. Soon after noon, my wife called me on the phone and said Esther was still worse. It seemed that she was having great difficulty in breathing, and that I should come home quickly. My brothers and the others in the office heard me phoning. I told them my message from the Lord, but they thought I must get a doctor, and they could

---

[b]J. Walter Malone, Jr., was superintendent of the Children's Country Training Home, and pastor of the Homewood (Illinois) Presbyterian Church and the McKinley Memorial Presbyterian Church (Champaign, Illinois), moderator of the Presbyterian Synod of Illinois, vice-president of McCormick Theological Seminary (Chicago), and president of Milliken College (Decatur, Illinois). For further data, see endnote 2.

[c]Esther Malone Waterbury was an executive with the Associated Charities of Cleveland and also with the Republic Steel Corporation. For further data, see endnote 3.

not see how I could dare to do without one.

I hastened immediately to go home. Just as I was standing on the corner waiting for the streetcar, Mrs. [Anna A.] Thompson, a dear saint of the Lord and a very dear friend of ours who had been miraculously healed of tuberculosis in its worst stages, had a home for divine healing, and was a member of our Friends Meeting, came up just as the car did.[5] I asked her to quickly get on the car and go home with me, for we needed help. This she immediately did without question.

When we reached home, I found the little daughter hanging as it were between life and death, unconscious, and lying in her mother's arms. We quickly prayed over her and anointed her with oil in the name of the Lord according to James 5:14, believing and trusting that she would be healed. Together we were enabled to pray the prayer of faith for her.

I picked up the child in my arms, wrapping her in a pair of warm blankets, and took her into the back parlor before the open fire, closing the door and holding her there before the Lord. She never moved a muscle all night long, until near the peep of day she began to move her hands a little, and said, "Papa, I's better." Oh what a joyful sound that was.

At 8:00 a.m. some of my brothers and their wives called with fearful hearts to see how she was doing. When they saw her on the blanket on the floor in front of the fire they exclaimed, "Well, we prayed and cried nearly all night at our house for fear she would die, for when we called last night and heard her breathing we thought she was dying." After this the presence of the Lord in the home was so manifest. We were glad we had trusted Him and had a well daughter. Everyone knew that the Lord had been there.

Emma's Vision

As I recall, it was more than a year or so later when our same daughter [Esther] had a severe attack of diphtheria. It seemed as if she would choke to death, but her mother and she were segregated from the rest of the family,[d] and prayed the case through until the great Physician manifested Himself, and just at the crucial hour He appeared to my dear faithful wife as One in the midst: the One for whose coming she had so faithfully held on in prayer. Her eyes were opened to see that He was with them in the room, and the little daughter at once coughed up all (the mucous membrane?). The fever had subsided, and she was immediately well. This happened in the year of the great Student Volunteer Convention [1898],[e] when William E. Blackstone, who wrote *Jesus Is Coming* [1878] and who is known for other prophetic teaching, was our guest in our home. He was in great travail of soul with us, and was glad to testify to this miracle of healing.[5] After this, the children were not only healed themselves, but they gladly and beautifully helped to pray the others through,[f] just as they had done with the little one [Esther] who was healed from diphtheria.

Some twenty years have gone by since that sacred hour.[g] Nevertheless, I still feel the thrill of Christ's presence when I recall that moment when He manifested Himself to my wife at the bedside of our daughter in our home.

---

[d]Emma Malone is remembered as a strong, yet tender, person. When someone was sick in the home, it was her custom to announce that she was "taking charge." Geraldine Osborne Williams (b. 1920), a grandaughter, recalls Emma Malone as a very nurturing grandmother.

[e]The Student Volunteer Convention met in Cleveland from February 23-27, 1898. The *Cleveland Plain Dealer*, 28 February 1898, p. 2 reported that "the convention has undoubtedly been the greatest gathering of the kind since the time when God bid his disciples go forth and preach the gospel in every land." For more data, see endnote 5.

[f]"Pray through" is a colloquialism used in "holiness" circles. It signifies a need to persevere in prayer until one experiences an internal certitude that the prayer has been answered.

[g]If - as Walter Malone tells us here - this manuscript was written some twenty years after 1898, which was the year in which the Student Volunteer Convention met in Cleveland, then this autobiography should be dated from the early to the mid-1920's, or before 1926 or 1927. After that time Walter Malone suffered so severely from Parkinson's disease (see Afterword) that he was scarcely able to write at all.

Walter's Healing

Once when I was so sick and my life was despaired of, my wife gathered the whole family together about my bed to pray for my healing. My wife prayed first as they knelt there, then the second son, and then each in turn, as was our custom according to age.

When it came to the little daughter's time to pray, the spirit of real intercession came upon her. She prayed as I had never heard a child pray before, nor have since. She pleaded for her father, saying the Church needed him, the Bible Institute needed him, his little family needed him. As she pressed her case before the Lord I felt the thrill of life power going through my body. Wife pressed my hands. I opened my eyes, and there the child was with her streaming eyes, with uplifted hands pleading her case as a real intercessor. She was on good terms with her Lord and Judge, and she went on pleading as to how Mother needed me, and how the boys needed their father, and how "we little girls need our Papa."[6] She prayed on and on until we all knew the prayer of faith had been prayed, and we were all weeping for joy and rejoicing that the great Physician had come. They knew I was healed and ready to get up.

Emma's Healing

One of the hardest tests of our faith came [in 1902] when my dear wife had her attack of bronchitis, which was of such a serious nature that we despaired of her life. It just seemed impossible for her to get her breath at all in any position. We asked interested friends who were known to prevail in prayer for the sick to come and pray. We gathered together and prayed at our home, and continued in prayer until later at night because our case was desperate.

One morning she said to me that she would like to have a specialist, a lung specialist by the name of Hoover.[7] It had been pressed upon her mind during the night, but who the doctor was, or where he lived, we had no idea. She felt the Spirit of the Lord had impressed the name upon her heart in the night. She felt the Lord was going to heal her, and she wanted the best specialist to testify as to her affliction, for she said time and again that this sickness was not for us but for a testimony to others.

Dr. Hoover was looked up and called for special diagnosis of the case. After what seemed to be a thorough examination, he told us that the tissue of her lungs had worn out and was like a worn out piece of rubber. The stretch was all gone out of it. It could not recoil or go back again. We would have to get some mechanical contrivance to be worked by arms to expel the air from the lungs. She could inhale, but could not exhale.

The doctor turned to me and said, "I don't know anything about you, Mr. Malone, or about your circumstances, but your wife can never again live in this climate. She possibly might live in the mountains of Colorado. I advise that you move at once, for I can do nothing for her." I said, "Thank you, Doctor, but our calling and work in business are all here by the will of the Lord. We will have to find a greater Physician than you." He went away and said "Malone is crazy."

There were a few more days of fasting and nights of prayer and waiting on the Lord, but one evening when I knelt at her bedside about ten o'clock, the King's sceptre was held out to me. The spirit of intercession was given, and there in the audience chamber of the King I tarried on my knees for two or three hours without fatigue or weariness and poured my heart's petition out to Him who I knew was hearing. I told wife to go to sleep. I would watch and pray, for I had the King's ear. Then she soon fell off into a restful sleep for the first time in days, if not for four or five weeks.

About midnight, or a little later, I felt relaxation and I lay down and rested about one-half an hour, and awoke just as if I had had an all night's sleep. I was at just the same place in prayer as when I lay down. Then all through the rest of the night and until morning the Spirit kept pouring through my heart and lips groanings that cannot be expressed in words. It was like spending a night in Heaven.

My wife awoke at the peep of day and began praising the Lord. Then she said something began to roll off her head and down her shoulders over her body and off at her feet, and the sickness was all over. Her lungs were perfectly healed, and she was well.[h]

---

[h]For a report of "severe Bronchial trouble" that left Emma Malone "very sick" for three months, see *The Soul-Winner*, Vol. 1 (16 January 1902), p. 34.

ENDNOTES

[1]Carroll Brown Malone (25 November 1886 - 16 February 1973) received an A.B. degree from Western Reserve University, Cleveland, Ohio, in 1908; an M.A. from the University of Michigan in 1909; taught physics at Tsinghua College in Peking, China, from 1911-1927; received an M.A. in history from Harvard University in 1920; and a Ph.D. in history from the University of Illinois in 1928. He was an associate professor at Oberlin College (Ohio) in 1928-1929; a professor at Miami University (Ohio) in 1929-1930; a professor and chair of the history department at Colorado College from 1930-1956; and a professor and chair of the history department at Tunghai University (Taiwan) from 1956-1959. For more data, see the Carroll B. Malone Collection at Colorado College, Colorado College Library, Colorado Springs, Colorado.

[2]J. Walter Malone, Jr., (4 March 1889 - 7 November 1962) a Phi Beta Kappa graduate from Western Reserve University in 1909, received a B.D. degree from McCormick Theological Seminary(Chicago) in 1919. In 1911 he became superintendent of the Children's Country Training Home near Amherst, Ohio, an extension of the ministry of Walter and Emma Malone that cared for 65 children, including schooling through high school and in six industrial trades. He married Elizabeth Mather Compton in 1914, served as pastor of the Presbyterian Church in Homewood, Illinois, from 1917-1922, and of the McKinley Memorial Presbyterian Church in Champaign, Illinois, from 1922-1941, where he organized the McKinley Foundation and the University of Illinois Student Center. He was the moderator of the Presbyterian synod of Illinois in 1927-28; vice-president of McCormick Seminary (Chicago) from 1941-1946, and president of Millikin University (Decatur, Illinois) from 1946-1956. The Malone Memorial Chapel and the J. Walter Malone Scholarship at Millikin are named for J. Walter Malone, Jr. For an obituary, see the Decatur *Herald and Review*, 8 November 1962.

[3]Esther (Malone) Waterbury (31 July 1890 - 4 June 1981) was a graduate of Oakwood Friends School and Wilmington College in Ohio (1912), worked as an executive with the Associated Charities of Cleveland, and "headed employee personnel at Republic Steel Corp. [Cleveland] during World War II, where she hired and supervised women." See the *Cleveland Plain Dealer*, 5 June 1981. She married Ralph Howard Waterbury in 1924.

[4]Mrs. Anna A. Thompson (1840-1902) was a daughter of Ezra Pearson, who was a Friend. In 1884 she opened a "Faith Home" in Erie, Pa., where faith healing was practiced. She came to Cleveland in 1886 and started an "Elim Home" for friendless children. Her obituary in the *Soul Winner*, 4 December 1902, credited her with being "instrumental in the healing of a great many very sick people."

[5]The Student Volunteer Movement was founded in 1876 at a summer missions conference organized by Dwight L. Moody in Northfield, Massachusetts. The mission of the movement was "the evangelization of the world in this

generation." The principal speakers at the Cleveland convention included F. B. Meyer, Robert Speer, and many seminary and college professors. Delia Fistler, a missionary to India and graduate of the Malones' school in Cleveland, also addressed the convention.

William Eugene Blackstone (1841-1935) spoke at the Ohio Yearly Meeting in August 1897, and at the Malones' Training School in December 1897. Blackstone, Eliza Armstrong (editor of the *Friends' Missionary Advocate*), President Rosenberger of Penn College, and Oscar Roberts (a Quaker missionary to Africa) spoke at the First Friends Church on 26 February 1898. Blackstone was a proponent of the dispensational premillennialism of John Nelson Darby which, at least in the later 19th century, challenged "civil religion" by dissenting from the popular and "modernist" view that progressive American culture would usher in the millennium.

To "modernists," who stressed immanence and not transcendence, the immanence of God meant that spiritual progress comes through the advance of Protestant democratic cultures. To premillenialists, no government or social system would be specially blessed by God until the coming of Christ's kingdom. In general, premillenialists abandoned this counter-cultural stance after the United States entered the 1st World War.

Blackstone, who in 1891 petitioned President Harrison to settle persecuted Russian Jews in Palestine, may have contributed to Walter and Emma Malone's sympathies for Jews in Romania, Russia, and the United States. For support for persecuted Jews, see *The Bible Student*, Vol. 27 (1897), pp. 12-13; *The Soul-Winner*, Vol. 1 (1902), p. 415; *The Soul-Winner*, Vol. 2 (1903), pp. 112-113, 326; *The Soul-Winner*, Vol. 3 (1904), p. 170; and *The Soul-Winner*, Vol. 4 (1905), pp. 277-78. In 1893 Lucy Ryder Meyer and Blackstone, who supported rescue mission work, were elected to the executive committee of the deaconesses conference of the Methodist Episcopal Church. See the *Cleveland Plain Dealer*, 27 February 1893, p. 5.

[6]This daughter was either Ruth or Margaret Malone. Ruth Malone married Byron L. Osborne, who was president of Malone College from 1951-1960. Margaret Malone edited the garden column of the *Cleveland Press*, and married Chester Crobaugh, a Cleveland financier. After Crobaugh's death, she married Atty. Luther Day, the president of the Cleveland Bar Association and a son of William R. Day (secretary of state under President William McKinley). Day's firm, now known as Jones, Day, Reavis, and Pogue, is presently the second largest law firm in the United States, with overseas offices in Brussels, Frankfort, Geneva, Hong Kong, London, Paris, Riyadh, Taipei, and Tokyo.

[7]The *Cleveland Directory* for 1902 lists a Dr. Charles F. Hoover, with an office in the Rose Building at 835 Case Avenue, and a Dr. Charles S. Hoover, who was a physician at Lakeside Hospital.

Chapter Ten

SPIRIT WORKING WITH OUR DOMESTIC HELP

"I ran away to get rid of being converted."

I remember one morning two Catholic girls who worked in our home came to my wife after worship and breakfast were over and the children had gone out to school.[a] They said that they would like to see her a few minutes in regards to the needs of their souls, for they felt themselves to be lost. They wanted to be saved, to give their hearts to God, and live Christian lives. After some questions and spiritual instructions, both were beautifully converted.

Lena Oberthier

After being saved, some helpers in our home took training in the Bible Institute, and afterwards became ministers and missionaries. One very striking girl, Lena [Magdalena] Oberthier, was a German who could barely speak English well enough to be understood when she was saved in a business meeting in the church one night.

She came at the invitation of a friend, who thought that we always had an altar service in our church, and who told me so at the door. As I was introduced to her by her friend, she said, "I hear you preach down here that one can be a Christian and live the holy life all the time." That evening we had a season of prayer in which she was wonderfully filled with the Spirit. The girl left rejoicing.

---

[a]It may help to recall here that Malone told us in Chapter 9 that "those assisting us in the home . . . [were] regularly asked into family worship, and some of them were converted from time to time."

After she returned to her room in her home where she was employed on Euclid Avenue, as I remember, she fell on her knees and began to pray for her brother, who was employed in another home five miles away. She never gave up praying until midnight, when she received assurance that God had saved her brother John.

The next morning John came to see her. He told her about the wonderful meeting he had had alone with God in his room at midnight, and how he was wondrously saved. Afterwards she became a helper in our home. One of the few times that tramps were welcome at our back door was while she was the cook in our kitchen.[b] As a rule she invited them in, fed them, prayed with them, preached to them, and often got them converted. Some turned up at the church and were saved.

The next Sabbath after she was saved, she had three German friends with her at the Sunday afternoon [Young People's] meeting. All were under conviction and were weeping. All three were beautifully saved. She persisted in seeking to get all her young friends and acquaintances to give their hearts to Christ, and her testimony always brought conviction.[1]

Not long after this, while Mrs. Malone and I were going away for a week of meetings, she decided to go away for the same time to help in a revival meeting with another young lady friend. She had wonderful results. Another time when we were out of town, she received an invitation from another young lady evangelist to go with her for several revivals, which she did. I have seen thousands of people crowding in to hear her preach in her broken German. Scores upon scores were converted at her meetings.

I remember one day when she came to Mrs. Malone and myself to ask us if she could go back to Germany to tell her family and folks and friends about this wonderful salvation, which she was sure that they had never heard about. The way was soon opened, and she went across to Germany. Revival after revival followed her in Germany.[2]

Not long after this she married an attorney in Germany who had some six or seven brothers. When her husband and she built their

---

[b]Byron Osborne, a son-in-law of the Malones and author of *The Malone Story*, told me that Walter Malone frequently invited persons who he encountered on the street to the Malone home for dinner. This apparently did not place an unwelcome burden on Emma Malone, perhaps in part because their meals were prepared and served by "domestic help."

new home, they constructed a room for their meetings in the upper story, where they had a real church service continually. In those meetings all of her brothers-in-law were converted except for one. He ran away from Germany and came to America to get away from his sister-in-law's preaching and messages. As I remember, four or five of her brothers-in-law became preachers, and all of them were very strong Christian workers.

A German professor from this country,[3] who was a beautiful Christian, stopped in Cleveland to see wife and me upon his return from Germany. He said that he bore love to my wife and myself from one whom he deemed to be one of the great women of Germany, a woman who had a church in her own home, and who was doing great good by having a great number of conversions. I was delighted to receive the news that it was Lena.

A Young Clergyman

Some few years later, as I was coming home on the train one Monday morning after being in meetings over the weekend, a fine looking young German stopped at my seat in the car as he was walking through to shake hands with me. He was wearing a little white preacher's necktie, and looked like a young clergyman.

He said, "Don't you know me, Brother Malone?" I had to confess I did not know him. "Why," he said, "I was converted in one of your prayer meetings on Cedar Avenue when you were there." I asked him his name, and he answered,

I am Lena Obertier's brother-in-law. I came from Germany because I could not live in Germany where Lena was without becoming a Christian. I ran away to get rid of being converted.

I came to Cleveland where I got so lonesome that I said to myself one night, "I will go around to the Friends Church where Lena used to go." I came to your prayer meeting, and while you were speaking I got under such conviction that I was glad to go forward for prayer and was wonderfully converted. I have just finished my theological schooling and been ordained as a minister of Jesus Christ. I am so glad to see you again and to tell you about it.

ENDNOTES

[1]Lena Oberthier applied for membership in the Cleveland Friends meeting on 19 November 1885, which was two months before the marriage of Walter and Emma Malone. Oberthier was living at that time at 869 Prospect Avenue.

[2]In August 1887 the Cleveland Friends Meeting sent a "minute of commendation to Lena Oberthier who is sojourning temporarily in Germany."

[3]The German professor may be Charles Lyttle, who was a professor of Church History at the Meadville Theological School, a Unitarian seminary founded at Meadville, Pennsylvania, in 1844, but which in 1936 was located in Chicago. Following the death of Walter Malone, Professor Lyttle wrote a letter of consolation to Walter Malone, Jr., in which he recounted memories of the personality and appearance of Walter Malone. The letter is dated 16 January, 1936, and is in the Malone College Archives. It reads in part as follows:

> Many, many years ago I used to go down to the old Friends' Church on Cedar Avenue in Cleveland with my good friends the Hinman family to worship, and I vividly recall the beautiful personality and spirit of your father and mother. I can still see them in memory's eye, sitting on the facing benches, your father always wearing a Prince Albert [coat] and white tie, and leading the service with such tender and uplifting prayers. . . . Cleveland, I am sure, has had few ministers more genuinely consecrated to Christ and more inspiringly influential upon young people than your father, and this letter is a tribute that I feel constrained to pay to his memory.

Chapter Eleven

THE SPIRIT WORKING IN OUR PASTORAL WORK

"You are Mr. Malone, the Quaker preacher. You always talk salvation to everybody."

I was once asked when I began to preach, and I said that I did not know. As a boy I found myself preaching to the chairs in the house, to the stock in the field, and to the chickens in our yard.

In school and in debate, I always felt I was to take God's side of the question. In business, I was known as - and sometimes called - the "Stone Man Preacher." My office in the Malone stone Company was called "the Prayer Meeting Room," for I talked with people as I did business with them. To our employees in the quarry and others with whom I met, I was always "the preacher." My business was to win souls for Jesus Christ. I was in the stone business to pay expenses.

In the church, I don't know when I became pastor of the flock. I don't know when I started. I arranged for the coming of ministers, and when each had to go, I arranged for another to come. As a rule I sat in our pulpit by their side, praying, planning, boosting, and saying "Amen."[a] I always felt that I was the messenger of the King, whether in the home, the church, or the business office. When traveling on the railroad, I hardly felt comfortable unless I was talking to someone about salvation.

---

[a]Elbert Russell, a professor of religion at Earlham and later chairman of the Divinity School at Duke University, reported on a Sunday dinner with the Malones in Cleveland in 1898. He complained that while the Malones "proved very gracious hosts, [nevertheless] their frequent emotional ejaculations - 'Praise the Lord,' 'Bless his name,' 'Hallelujah' - were novel and at times a little disconcerting." See Elbert Russell, *Elbert Russell: Quaker. An Autobiography* (Jackson, Tennessee: Friendly Press, 1956), pp. 95-96.

Pastoring on the Train

As an illustration, one day I was coming home from Chicago on the Lake Shore Railroad Limited. While I was having a good time with my Bible, the newsboy kept insisting on giving me some books to read. After a little while, I told him that I wanted to see and chat with him for a few minutes. I saw that he was not inclined to visit with me, but I insisted that he sit down with me. He said, "No, I don't care to. I know you. You are Mr. Malone, the Quaker preacher. You always talk salvation to everybody." However, I insisted that he sit down with me, and he finally said that he would join me after he had gone through the car one more time.

This he did, and when he sat down beside me I opened the question of his salvation as pleasantly as I could. He soon melted down until I saw that it was a good time to have a word of prayer with him. I slipped my arm around him and got him to bow his head. As I talked to him, he broke down in tears. I asked him to pray after I had led in prayer, and while we sat in the seat. I insisted on his praying, which after I put a few words in his mouth, he did. Then I prayed again and thanked God that He was willing to save this young man, forgive him, and make him a Christian. I told him that God loved him, Jesus had died for him, and God had a job in His vineyard for him. It was not very long until the light broke in as the witness of the Spirit came to him, and he was wonderfully converted. Afterwards he became a student at the Cleveland Bible Institute where he became a preacher. At last report, he was in the Northwest having a revival.

Another illustration. One Monday morning I took the train in Oklahoma for St. Louis. After two or three days of meetings where so many were wonderfully saved and sanctified, I was very tired and weary. I took a tourist's chair next to the window, and after resting a little while I opened my Bible to have my morning Quiet Hour.

The car kept filling up, but no one seemed to care to sit by a man with an open Bible.[b] I whispered in my prayer to the Lord that I would not mind it if no one sat by me because I was very tired. But not long after this, a tall, medium-weight miner came into the car. He

---

[b]Malone's willingness to be dismissed as an eccentric for the sake of "winning souls" is - in my view - one of the more significant indexes of his character.

had a pack under one arm, and his pants were tucked into his boots. Looking every inch a miner, he came and sat down by me.

I did not speak to him until I felt the Spirit whisper the words to my heart, "Thee had better speak to this man. It may be an opportunity." So I passed the compliments of the day to him, even though I saw that he did not feel like talking to me. I tried to open the conversation, but he seemed to try to avoid it. However, when I asked him where he was from and where he was going, he turned to me, told me a little about the mining in which he had been engaged, and we got into a conversation.

Finally I asked him if he was a Christian. He said "no," cutting me off rather short. But the Spirit helped me as I pressed the question of his personal salvation. I saw that I had hit the right spot in his heart when I asked him where he was from and where he was going. Soon he said to me,

> Stranger, you say that you are interested in my soul's salvation. I will tell you that I was just running away from home, leaving my wife and children to go up north to try my fortune again. I can't lead a decent life in my home town, nor can I live decently with my family. I am leaving them to try life in a different place.

"But," I said,

> don't you know that the devil and sin are up where you are going just the same as where you have been? What you need is a new heart and a new disposition. The Lord has promised to give us both if we will forsake our sins and ask Him.

I suggested that we bow our heads on the chair in front of us, and ask God to forgive and cleanse. I slipped my arm around him as he bowed his head, and there on that train while we were flying from Oklahoma I thought it was a good time to get this man saved. I prayed and put words in his mouth, which he finally prayed. Then I taught him how to appropriate his pardon. I prayed again and got him to pray some more. Suddenly he broke out in tears, and the Spirit took hold of him and transformed him into a new creature. After this he turned to me and said, "But stranger, what will I do now?" I said,

> I think if I were you that I would go back home and live for God and for my family. I would get the Bible and begin to read and pray with

my wife and children and be a blessing for Holiness in your community. God will stay by you.

He said, "I believe I will." Then he asked, "Should I get off at the next station and go back?" I told him, "I believe that I would." So, when the train stopped at the next station, he picked up his pack and got off the train so as to wait for the down train back home. He was a new creature in Christ Jesus.

Pastoring in the Home

Our home was a place where people who were under conviction continually came day and night to get saved. For instance, one Saturday night at about 9:00 p.m., after the family had gone to bed and I had gone upstairs after locking the house, the door bell rang. I went to the door and was met by a sorrowful looking man who said that he wanted to see me for a few minutes.

I invited him into the living room where I asked him to be seated, and inquired as to his trouble. He said,

The other day you walked through the factory where I work, and I thought that you looked at me and said in your heart, "I wonder if he is a Christian." From that hour I have been miserable. I said I would come over and see you, but I put it off until the last thing Saturday night. I am a deacon in our church, and have been for ten years. Yet I have never known my sins to be forgiven and my heart cleansed as you teach, for I have heard you preach. I made up my mind that I would not go another Sunday and serve in our church and not be a Christian. I have come at this late hour to ask you to help me through.

I was very much delighted to do this. He was easily led into the fountain for sin and uncleanness, and he went out a happy man to serve the church in his capacity.

Another illustration, and an interesting one that also happened

in our home. In the days when the Keeley cure[c] was so much advertised and worked to cure drunkards, a rather nice looking man came
by one morning at about 9 or 10 a.m. to ask for a conference. He said
that he was a poor man and wanted me to help him. He had lost his
job time and again, and was a public failure from drink. He said that
he had gone down to the Keeley cure to see if they could help him,
but they had said that they would not treat him unless he got Mr.
Malone to sign his recommendation.

As he pulled his paper out of his pocket, I said to him "You
mean that you have such trouble with drink that you have lost your
job, ruined your reputation, spoiled your family circle, and cannot stop
drinking?" He said, "Yes, Mr. Malone. My only hope is the Keeley
cure. Won't you please sign my recommendation?"

"But, said I, "if you take the Keeley cure, and it fixes you so that
you do not drink, you will be just as bad a man as before, except for
drink. I don't believe it is the Keeley cure that you need for your
case."

"Oh," he said, "please sign it for me. I don't know what else to
do. I am ruined unless I get it." And he pleaded with me to sign his
paper.

I said, "I have not refused to sign your paper. But I want to
diagnose your case. What you need isn't a cure for one sin, drink. You
need a cure for all sins that makes a new man, a new heart, a new
disposition."

"Well," he said, "I would like to have that too. But I am
desperate to be cured from drink."

"But," I said, "drink is only one sin, nor is it all your troubles.
What will you do about the other sins?"

He replied, "I don't know, but I will try and do better if you will
just sign my application."

Then I said, "But suppose we try the blood cure, for the blood
of Jesus Christ cleanses from ALL SIN. Isn't that what you need?"

He replied, "That is what I need, of course. But I am too sinful
for that just now."

---

[c]The Keeley Cure was named for Dr. Leslie E. Keeley of Cleveland. In 1892
the Keeleyites organized "The Keeleyite Bi-Chloride of Gold Club of the State of
Ohio." Keeley predicted that "in twenty years not a saloon will be left in the United
States." See the *Cleveland Plain Dealer*, 3 September 1892, p. 6.

Then I slipped my arm around him and said,[d] "Let's pray over it, and ask God to forgive you of all sin, and cleanse your heart from all unrighteousness." Then he knelt with me as I prayed, and at last I got him to pray. The Lord answered our petitions, gave him a new heart, and took away the old stony heart. He was a new creature.

Finally he arose, praising the Lord for his deliverance. He took the Keeley application, handed it to me, and said, "This is not what I want or what I need. I have just received what I wanted and needed in Jesus Christ." After a little while, he left my home praising God.

I don't remember whether it was a week or two later, but on a Monday morning a man drove up to our home in a business wagon with another man beside him, whom I recognized to be the man who had wanted the Keeley cure so badly. He brought his comrade to the front door and introduced him to me saying, "My friend, Jim Blake, wants to see you for a few minutes. I am in a hurry, so excuse me. I will leave Jim with you."

I took him in the living room, and said, "Jim, what can I do for you?" He answered, "I am in the same trouble that Bill was in when he came to see you a couple of weeks ago, and was cured." "What," said I, "Are a drunkard too?" He replied,

> Yes sir, I am out of a job and out of a home, and I don't know what in the world to do. When I saw the change in Bill's life, the transformation in his home, and all, I asked him what happened, and he told me the story of the Keeley cure and the blood cure at your house, and asked me if I would like to go out and see you.

I asked, "What did it do for Bill?" He said, "It has changed his whole life. It changed his home into a heaven and got him a good job in which he is now making money and doing nicely. He goes to church, takes his family, reads his Bible, and prays at home."

"Well," I said, "if you want that, you can get it right here at the sofa where Bill got his." We then knelt together where his friend Bill had found salvation. Jim too was transformed by the power of God.

---

[d]It was Malone's custom to "slip his arm" around persons for whom he was praying, a practice that may have begun while doing mission work in Cleveland. It was also his practice to call an individual aside, embrace him or her, and then whisper to that person, "You know, don't you, that the Lord and I are counting on you?"

AFTERWORD BY BYRON LINDLEY OSBORNE, JR.[a]

REMEMBERING MY GRANDFATHER

**"I have seen a great multitude . . . gathered around a throne.
. . . And I know a great many of them!"**

My grandfather Malone was the most powerful spiritual influence in my early life. A retired Quaker minister, broken in health, he lived with us the first thirteen years of my life: 1922-1935.

The most moving recollection that I have as a child is leading that frail, holy man, who could not walk alone, into the sunroom of our home to prop him up on a couch so that he could read his Bible and pray.

I used to watch him as he read the Bible. In a very few minutes his face would light up as if in a trance, and he would begin a gentle outburst that was somewhere between laughing and crying. When I was very young, I thought that happened to everybody when they read the Bible. Only later did I begin to see this man's extraordinary sensitivity.

There was a gentle mysticism that pervaded his entire life. Although he was crippled with Parkinson's disease, and shook with what they then called "palsy," and was in continuing pain, I never saw him complain or lose his kindness. And only once did I ever hear him raise his voice, and that was at me once when I got mad at my sister; and I remember that it broke my heart.

Perhaps the climax of his life for me was his death. It was an old-fashioned death-bed scene. His family had been called, and we were all around his bed just before he died. He had been in a coma when suddenly his face lit up as it had on so many occasions when I had seen him read his Bible and pray.

---

[a]Byron Lindley Osborne, Jr., is a grandson of Walter and Emma Malone and a professor of world religions and director of Theater 360 at Brevard Community College in Florida. Osborne is a graduate of Cleveland Bible College, Yale University Divinity School (B.D. and S.T.M.), and Concordia Seminary (Th.D.) in St. Louis. He wrote this tribute to his grandfather in 1990.

My father bent over him and using the reverent language of the Quakers asked him: "Father, what does thee see?" After he had been roused and brought back to waking consciousness, he tried with great difficulty to speak. He was trying to tell us that he had had a vision.

This is my recollection of his words: "I have seen a great multitude," he said, "gathered around a throne." And after struggling so hard to speak, he lapsed back into his coma. But my father pressed him again to share with us one more time. And rallying, he came back and with great difficulty spoke his last words. He recalled what he had just said: "I have seen a great multitude gathered around a throne." Then, as if gazing at them, he added: "And they are clothed in white!" And finally, as if joining them, he whispered: "And I know a great many of them!" And he was gone.

With this vision of glory he left us. But not really, because for those of us who knew him intimately, the benediction of his life has haunted us all of our lives, and, we hope, will haunt our children all of their lives and their children to the end of time.

INDEX

Soon after the beginning of this work the question of finance came on. I did not like to ask people for money, but I needed it for Sunday School papers, song books and the like. So I was very definitely led to pray for the Lord to bless the store business so that I should pray for the needs of the Sunday School and the Young People's meeting. Of course I had prayed much over the business since going into the office and the work was very perceptibly picking up and going much better. I was led out into prayer for more store orders and for collections to come in, and it was for the Sunday School and Young People's meetings?". And it seemed to me as if I had no secular work. It was all for God and His work. I was in the store business to pay expenses to further the religious work.

One day with the office door locked while in prayer and reading my little pocket Bible, I knew not how, but I was led to the story of the twenty-eighth chapter of Genesis where the Lord so graciously met Jacob that night on the plain so far from home and from mother, and God gave him a new start in life. And I followed Jacob in his prayer and promise, identifying with him and reading each sentence of his vow to God, and then making it my own prayer. It was my meaning in prayer that morning.

> If the Lord will be with me, and will keep me in the way that I go,
> and will give me bread to eat and raiment to put on, so that I come
> again to my father's house in peace, then shall the Lord be my God:
> And this stone, which I have set for a pillar, shall be God's house: and
> of all that thou shalt give me I will surely give the tenth unto thee.
> [Genesis 28:10-22]

I went through the verses, underlining each part until I came to and last clause of the last verse, "And of all that thou shalt give me I surely will give the tenth to Thee." Here I paused and was face to face with the tithing question for the first time in my life that I could recall. I had never heard it discussed, that I know of, nor knew anybody who did it. I was asking finances of the Lord, and He asked me to recognize His

_____

(continued)

support and interest on behalf of Anglo-Americans. This was one of the first Quaker
meetings which attracted first-rate young men, business men, Anglos and the urban
poor into membership.